Native American
DESIGNS·2

American Quilter's Society
P.O. Box 3290 • Paducah, KY 42002-3290
www.AmericanQuilter.com

Joyce
Mori

Located in Paducah, Kentucky, the American Quilter's Society (AQS) is dedicated to promoting the accomplishments of today's quilters. Through its publications and events, AQS strives to honor today's quiltmakers and their work and to inspire future creativity and innovation in quiltmaking.

EDITOR: SHELLEY HAWKINS
COPY EDITOR: CHRYSTAL ABHALTER
GRAPHIC DESIGN: AMY CHASE
COVER DESIGN: MICHAEL BUCKINGHAM
QUILT PHOTOS: CHARLES R. LYNCH

Library of Congress Cataloging-in-Publication Data

Mori, Joyce.
   Native American designs 2 / by Joyce Mori.
        p. cm.
   Summary: "More than one hundred authentic patterns representing a wide range of Native American cultures for traditional, contemporary and ethnic quiltmaking"-- Provided by publisher.
   ISBN 1-57432-895-6
   1. Quilting--Patterns. 2. Quilts--Themes, motives.   3. Indian art--North America.
   I. Title: Native American designs two. II. Title

   TT835.M6835 2005
   746.46'041--dc22

                              2005018211

Additional copies of this book may be ordered from the American Quilter's Society, PO Box 3290, Paducah, KY 42002-3290, or call 1-800-626-5420 or online at www.AmericanQuilter.com.

DEDICATION

This book is dedicated to my parents, Jessie Lee and Robert Newell, who raised me in a home where quilts were appreciated. They encouraged me to try different crafts and creative pursuits, and I have enjoyed the creative process throughout my life.

ACKNOWLEDGMENTS

I wish to thank the American Quilter's Society for its continued support of my work, and especially Meredith Schroeder for the commitment to reprint the two books I authored on Native American quilting designs. I thank all the quilters who are interested in using these designs for their quilting. Without you, my books would not be published.

Theresa Fleming of Colorado has converted some of my designs into patterns suitable for machine quilters and I appreciate her work.

My husband, John, receives my thanks and love for giving me support so that I may pursue my love of quilting.

Since the publication of my first book, my daughter, Susan, has taken up quilting and she has become an important sounding board for my ideas. I appreciate her feedback and enthusiasm.

Special thanks is given to all the anonymous Indian craftworkers and artisans who provided the legacy of design that I used to create these quilting motifs.

CONTENTS

INTRODUCTION

My first two books, *Quilting Patterns from Native American Designs* and *Native American Designs for Quilting,* are out of print, so many quilters have not been able to access those designs. In this publication, I have selected favorite designs from the two books with a goal of representing all the areas of the United States.

There are over a dozen new bonus patterns, plus a wall quilt project that provides large, open blocks for featuring several quilting motifs. The center block features a quilting design that has been adapted for machine appliqué. The designs in this book have been inspired by many Native American cultures, even prehistoric ones. The motifs came from pottery, rugs, beadwork, silverwork, woodwork, etc. Where possible, the designs have been identified as to tribe or region.

The two types of designs contained in this book include individual motifs that can be used as is or manipulated to create more complex quilting designs, and designs that have already been created from separate motifs. The latter type can be reworked by adding other motifs to it, as well as adding or subtracting lines.

The patterns are meant to be springboard designs that can be modified and adapted to fit each quilter's own needs. There is a section that illustrates how the separate motifs can be used to create new and more complex quilting designs (page 8). To spur creativity, some of the separate motifs feature a small drawing that shows one way to use the motif to create a more complex unit.

Quilting is the last major step in the process of completing a quilt. It is the last chance to add more beauty or reinforce a theme, so I hope you find many patterns in the following pages to enhance your works of art. These designs can be used on any type of quilt – traditional, contemporary, or ethnic. They are timeless, unique, and adaptable.

These patterns do not have to be limited to just quilting motifs. Many can be used as appliqué motifs, including wool appliqué. They can be converted into quilt labels; there is a group of these specially designed as such (page 101). They can be used as embroidery designs or designs to be colored with fabric paints or crayons. I hope you enjoy experimenting with these ideas.

TRACING QUILTING DESIGNS ON FABRIC

The technique you use to transfer quilting patterns to fabric can vary with each project or design. If possible, I like to transfer the design to my quilt top before I baste the layers. However, you do not want the traced design to wear off before you quilt, so you may want to transfer only a portion of the design as you go.

The type of marking device you use can influence when you mark the design. The advantage of transferring the design before layering the quilt is that you do not have to make a stencil from the design. Instead, simply photocopy the design and use an *indelible* pen to connect all the dashes, making a dark, solid line. Place this copy over a light source and under your quilt top, then trace the design on the fabric using your favorite washout pen or pencil.

If you are using this method with a complex design, I suggest copying the design onto freezer paper. Draw the design with a black *permanent* pen on the freezer paper's unwaxed side. This makes it easier to see the design through the fabric. Then iron the freezer paper on the wrong side of the quilt and trace the motif. The freezer paper keeps the fabric from shifting, especially when you have to trace many lines. I use a washout cloth marker for tracing, but you can use whatever marking pen or pencil you are comfortable with. I usually trace the design from the top to the bottom to keep my hands off previously traced areas.

In some cases, only half or a quarter of a large design is provided because of page size limitations. You will need to lift and re-iron the freezer paper two or four times to complete the tracing of the entire design.

For designs that do not have much detail in the center, you can trace the outline of the motif onto clear plastic and cut it out. You can then use the cutout as a stencil for tracing the design's outer edges on fabric. Even if the design has some interior lines, they can often be drawn freehand just before you quilt the motif. While making a stencil is more time consuming than tracing a design, it is advisable if you are going to use the same design many times on a quilt. You can also loan the stencil to friends, or have it as a permanent part of your stencil collection.

If you make a stencil for more complex designs, I recommend using a hot stencil gun. It quickly and easily burns the channels needed. I have also found that a leaded-glass pattern cutter with a double blade works well for cutting channels. The special template plastic recommended for use with the cutter makes the stencils easy to cut.

When using stencils, you need a device for marking in the channels. I have used a washout marker, pencil, or soapstone marker that fits into a pencil-like holder. I have also had success with a transfer or pounce pad filled with chalk powder. When the pad is wiped over the stencil, the powder goes through the channels to mark the design. The lines made with the last two devices rub off easily, so you will want to mark each area only as you are getting ready to quilt.

Suggested Materials

light source for tracing • black permanent pen
freezer paper • clear plastic
washout marker, pencil, or pounce pad
access to a photocopier

Workshop teachers and your own experience will lead you to select a method of transferring designs that works for you. Be willing to try new products on the market. I do not find one procedure superior to others. The method I select depends on the specific design and the nature and color of the fabric.

Keep in mind that the designs can be reduced or enlarged with a copy machine to make them fit a particular space.

CREATIVITY WITH QUILTING DESIGNS

*A*ltering the designs is not difficult and can be a lot of fun. Just study the following illustrations to guide you through the process.

On a sheet of paper, draw a line from top to bottom in the middle of the sheet. Then draw a line perpendicular to the first one across the center of the page, again in the middle of the sheet (fig. 1). Make at least 10 copies of the sheet.

Make four copies of a motif from this book. Cut out the motifs, leaving about ⅛" of paper around the outside edge (fig. 2).

Now, you can begin to manipulate this motif. A light box is handy, but any source of backlight, such as a window, patio door, or glass-top table, will do. Use tape to hold two opposite corners of the paper against the glass. Place a motif in each of the four quadrants in different configurations as illustrated (figs. 3–9, pages 8–10).

Fig. 2.
Birchbark Design (Northeast Woodlands)

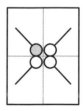

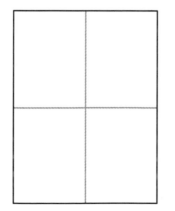

Fig. 1. Quadrant-marked paper

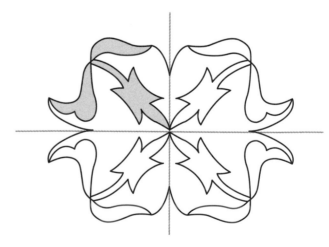

Fig. 3. Birchbark variation 1

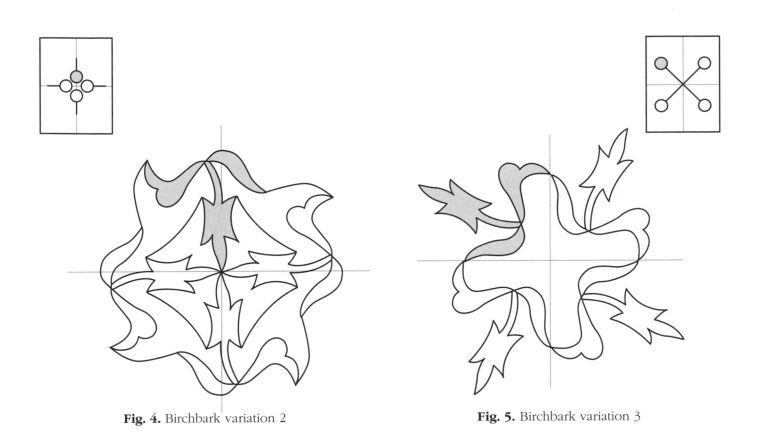

Fig. 4. Birchbark variation 2

Fig. 5. Birchbark variation 3

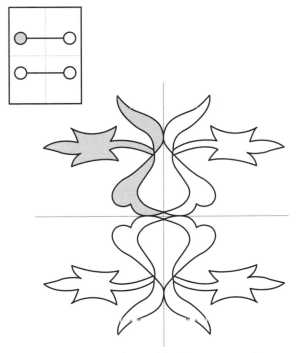

Fig. 6. Birchbark variation 4

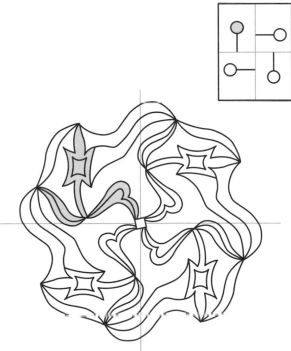

Fig. 7. Birchbark variation 5

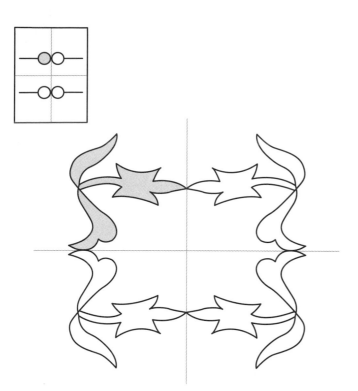

Fig. 8. Birchbark variation 6

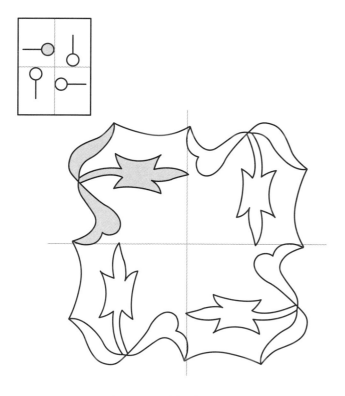

Fig. 9. Birchbark variation 7

After arranging the motifs, draw any pleasing arrangements on fresh pieces of quadrant-marked paper. Put all your new designs in a file folder. Even if you do not have a use for them at the moment, you may be able to use them in a future project.

You have just created new quilting motifs. That was certainly not difficult. Not all designs are pleasing in all arrangements, but a design can usually be manipulated in several ways to make new and attractive patterns.

A design can often be turned 90 degrees to create a more pleasing result (fig. 10, page 11). In figures 3 and 4 on pages 8 and 9, the motif was rotated 45 degrees until the design was oriented on the quadrant lines, which changes the appearance. Extra connecting lines were added to both variations.

The previous examples show a motif in a four-quadrant alignment. You can also try six- and eight-quadrant alignments. Many of the designs offer potential for further adaptations. You can enlarge or reduce your newly created designs on a copy machine. You can also enlarge or reduce a single motif before using it in new arrangements.

Once you have created a design you like, there are even more changes you can make. If you want the design to fill a smaller space, you can eliminate some lines or use only a portion of the motif (fig. 11, page 11).

If you want the new design to fill a larger space, there are some easy options. You can enlarge the design with a copy machine. Changing the size of a design on a copy machine may take more than one try. Have a ruler with you so you can measure the design at each stage of reduction or enlargement. Don't enlarge your design too much. If you want it to fit a 10" block, make it about 9¼" across to avoid placing the design in the seam allowances. It is much easier to quilt through three layers (top, batting, and backing) than five (top, batting, backing, and two seam allowances). If you need to enlarge the design beyond the size of the paper, you may have to enlarge it in sections and tape the pages together.

Once the design has been enlarged, it may be fine the way it is, or it may have too much empty space to suit you. In the latter case, you will need to add lines, depending on how much actual quilting you want to do. Extra lines were added to the motif in figure 7 on page 9 to fill in the empty space. Some other points to consider: Are you quilting just to hold the layers of the quilt sandwich together? Do you want the quilting to reinforce the total quilt design or to be the main design in a wholecloth quilt?

The more lines you add, the more the original design is lost, which is generally not a problem. You have, in effect, created a new design. If it's important to you to keep the emphasis on the original design, you can quilt it with a thread that is a different color from the extra lines. You can also use outlining to help preserve the integrity of the original motif, adding an extra line of quilting about ⅛" to ¼" around the outside of the motif (fig. 12).

There are some other creative options you can try with individual motifs (fig. 13, page 12). What would happen if part of the birchbark design were cut away? Could it be used that way? Perhaps parts of the motif can be made to fit into a triangular rather than square shape (fig. 14, page 12). Can the design be separated into parts? If so, perhaps one of the parts could be enlarged, another one could be reduced, and the unit could then be put back together. Be open to trying different design options. Don't be discouraged if every variation does not look great. Experiment and enjoy yourself in the process.

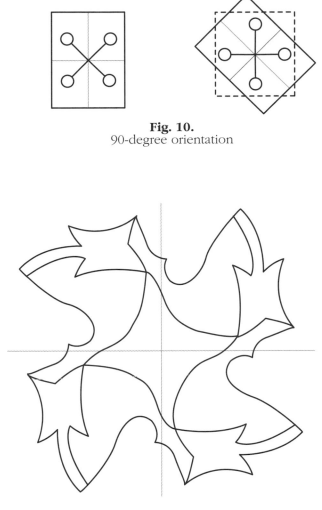

Fig. 10.
90-degree orientation

Fig. 11.
Design with a portion of the motif

Fig. 12.
Outlining a motif

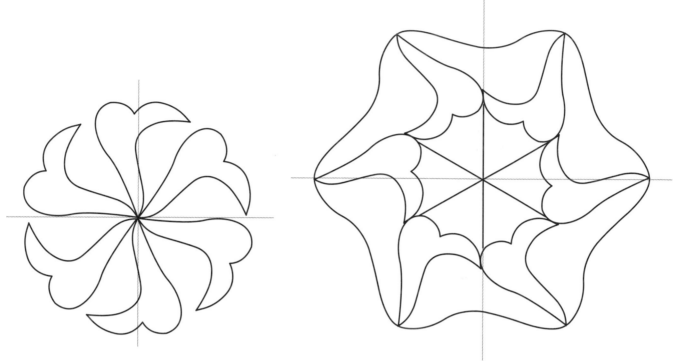

Fig. 13.

Design variations on a motif

Fig. 14.

Motif in a triangular shape

WORKING WITH A MOTIF

Cree Quillwork

Northwest Coast

MOTIFS AND DESIGNS

Southwest Area
Full design

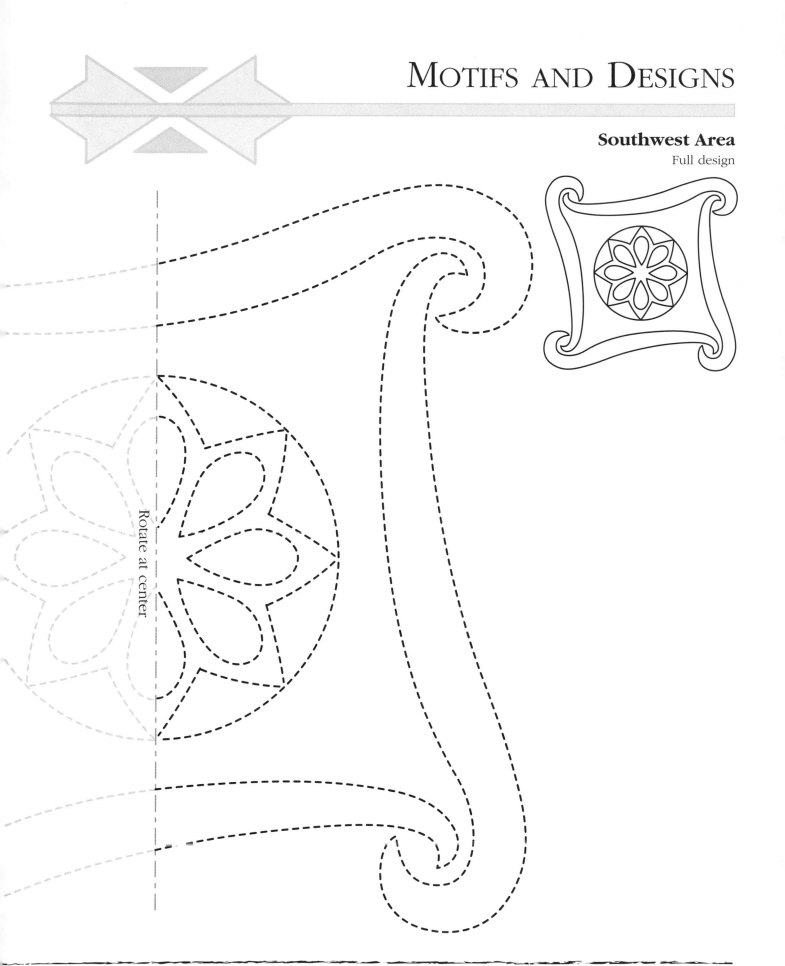

Rotate at center

Southwest Basketry

Full design

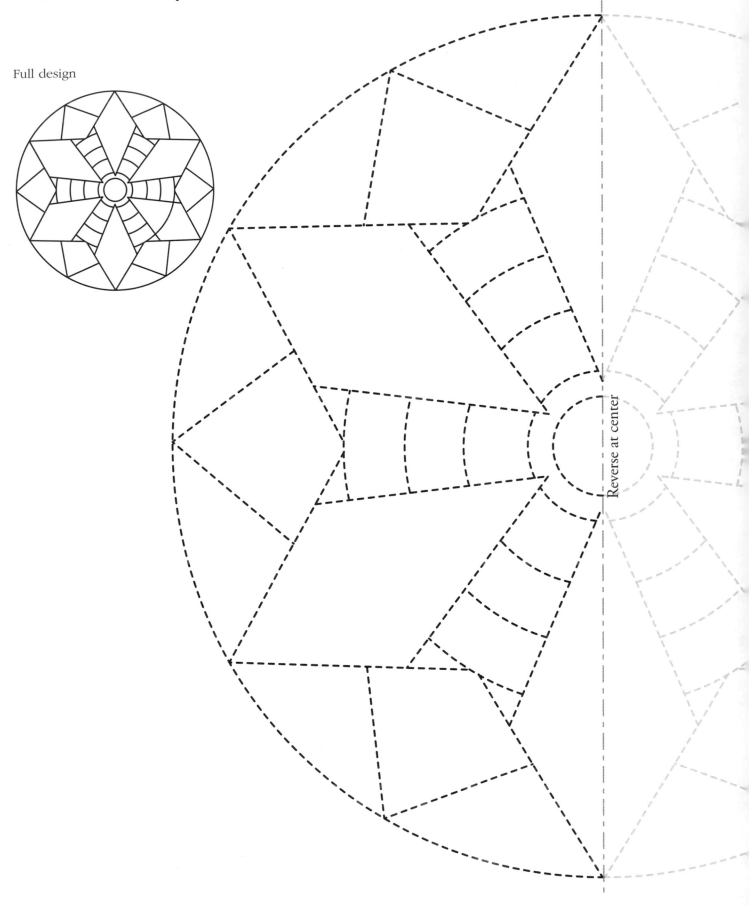

Reverse at center

Apache (Southwest) Basketry

Full design

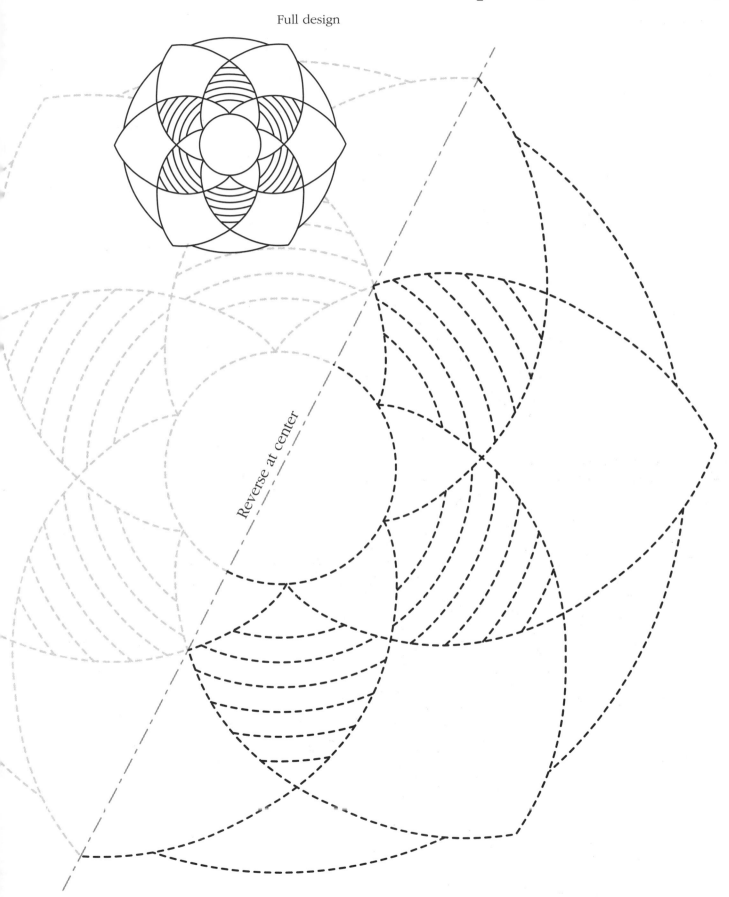

Reverse at center

Southwest Pottery

Full-size motifs for a 24" pattern
as shown below

Native American Snowflake Wholecloth Pattern

Full design

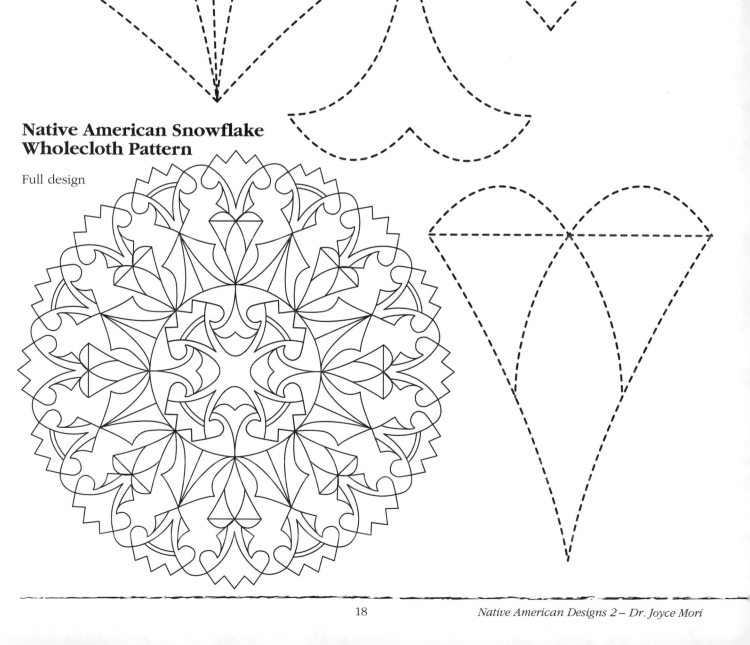

Apache (Southwest) Area

Reverse at center

Full design

Southwest Area

Full design

Rotate at center

Southwest Area

Rotate at center

Full design

Pima (Southwest) Basketry

Full design

Reverse at center

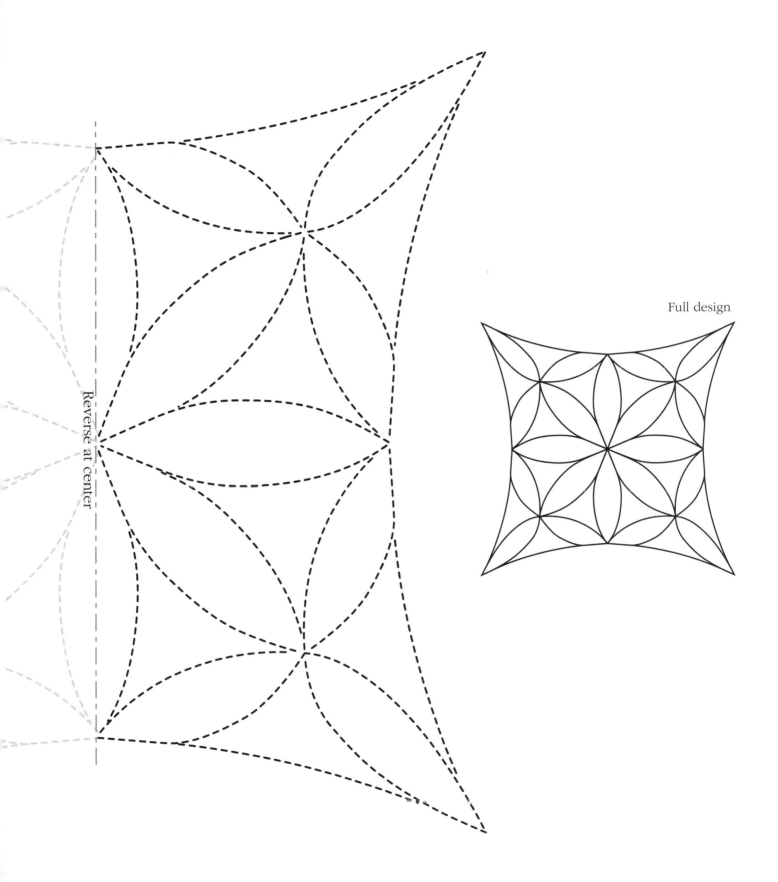

Full design

Reverse at center

California/Great Basin Area Basketry

Full design

Reverse at center

San Ildefonso (Southwest) Pottery

Southwest Area

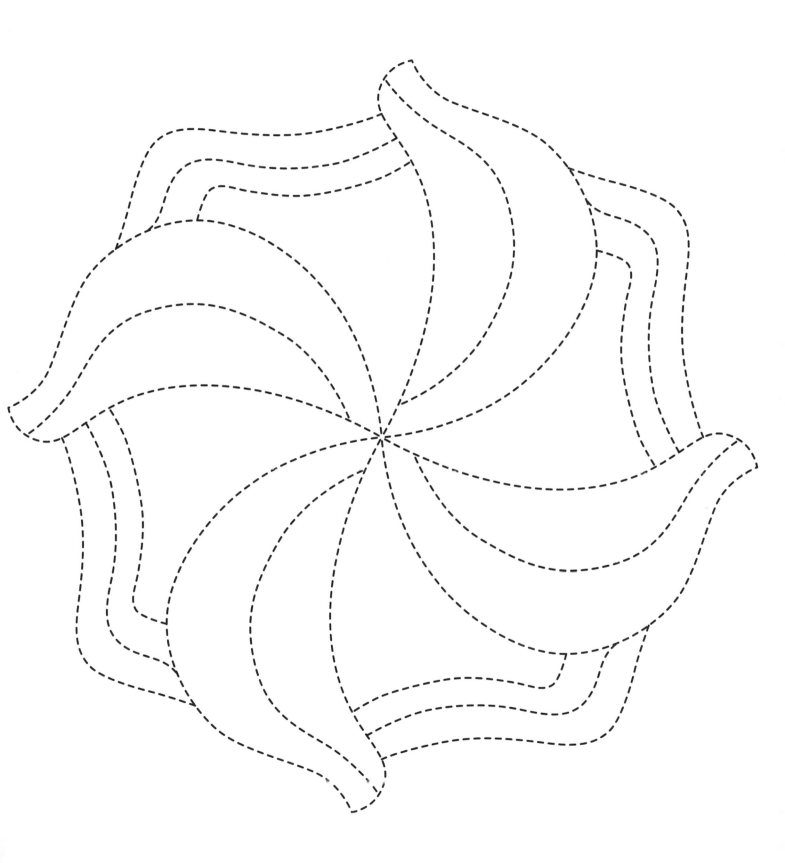

Southwest Pottery

Southwest Silverwork

Navajo (Southwest) Silverwork

San Ildefonso (Southwest) Pottery

Southwest Pottery

Full design

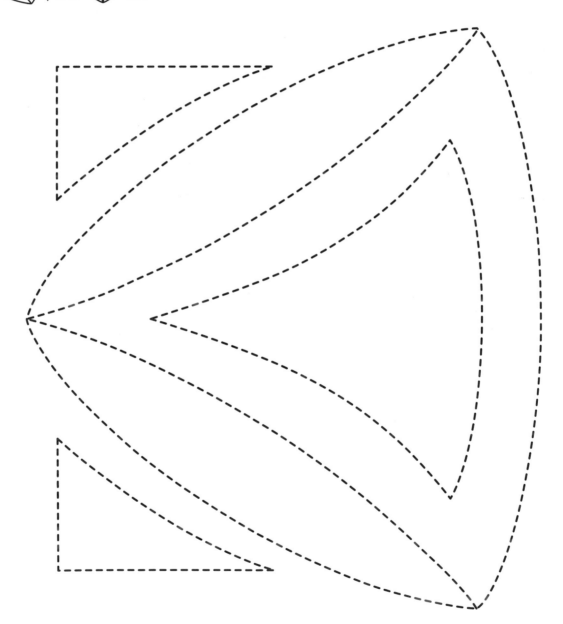

Zia (Southwest) Pottery

Zia Pottery

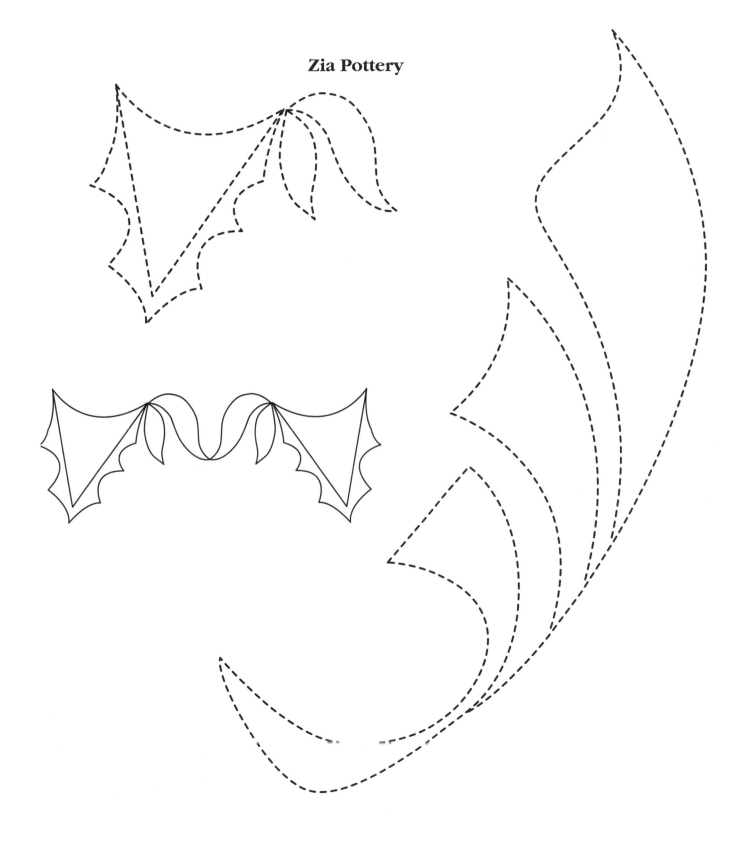

Kiowa (Plains)

Beadwork, late 1800s

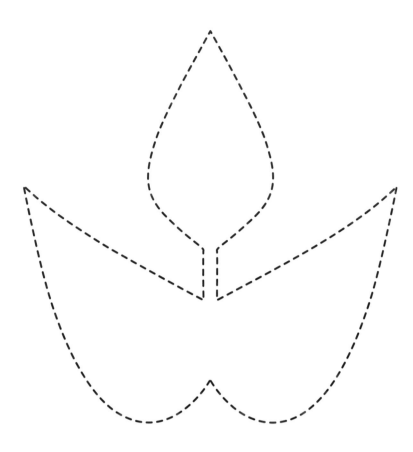

Southwest Silver

Southwest Jewelry

Ojibwa (Northeast Woodland) Beadwork

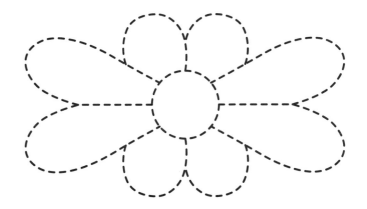

Unknown

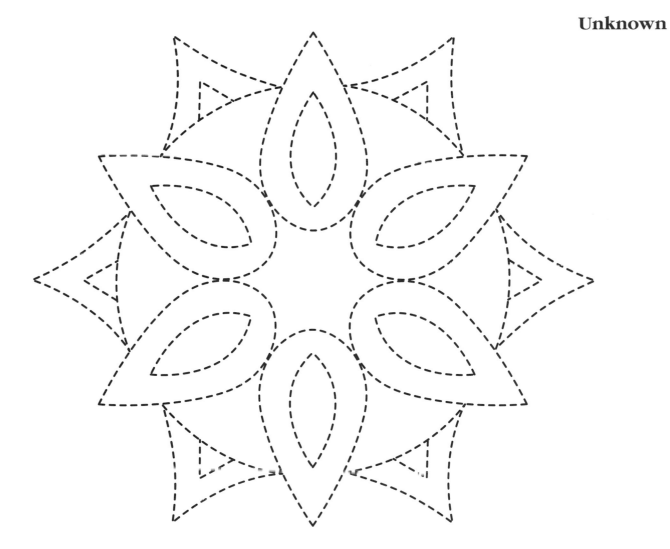

Southwest Pottery

Southwest Pottery

Full design

Crow (Plains) Parfleche

Southwest Silverwork

Northwest Coast Area

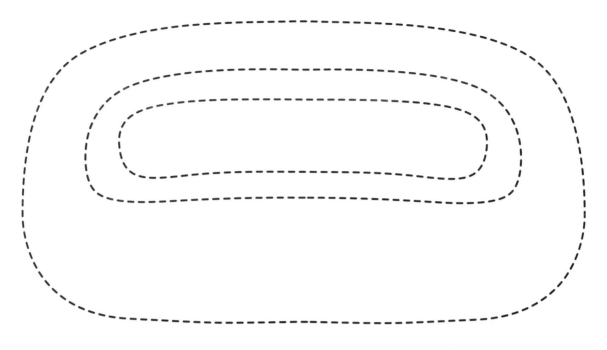

Ojibwa (Northeast Woodland) Beadwork

Navajo (Southwest) Silverwork

Navajo (Southwest) Silverwork

Southwest Pottery

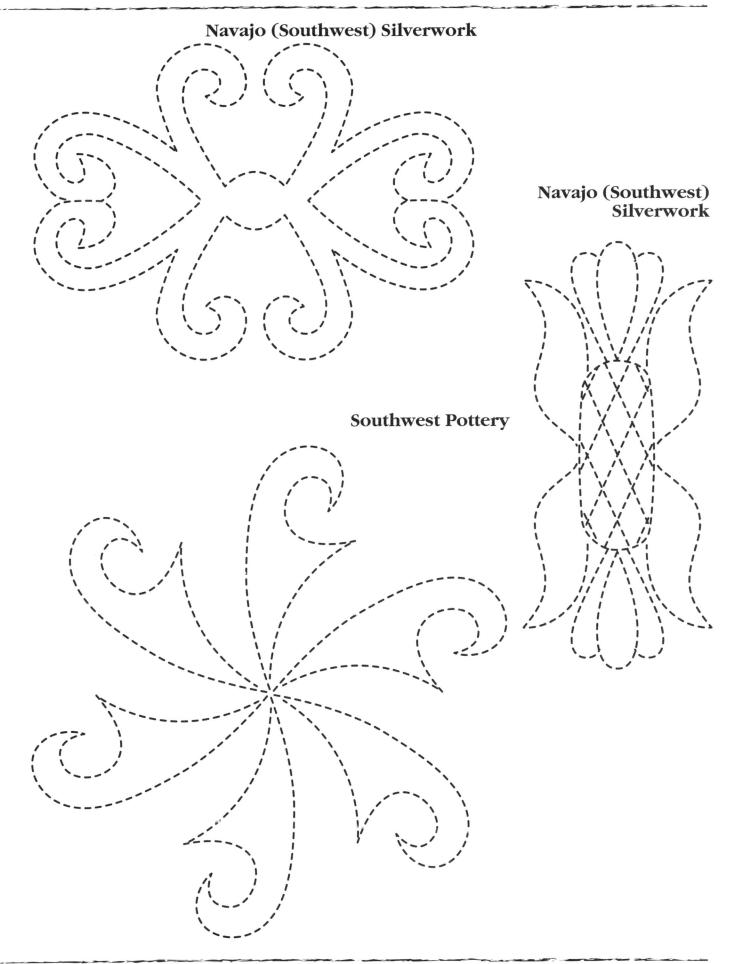

Southwest Design

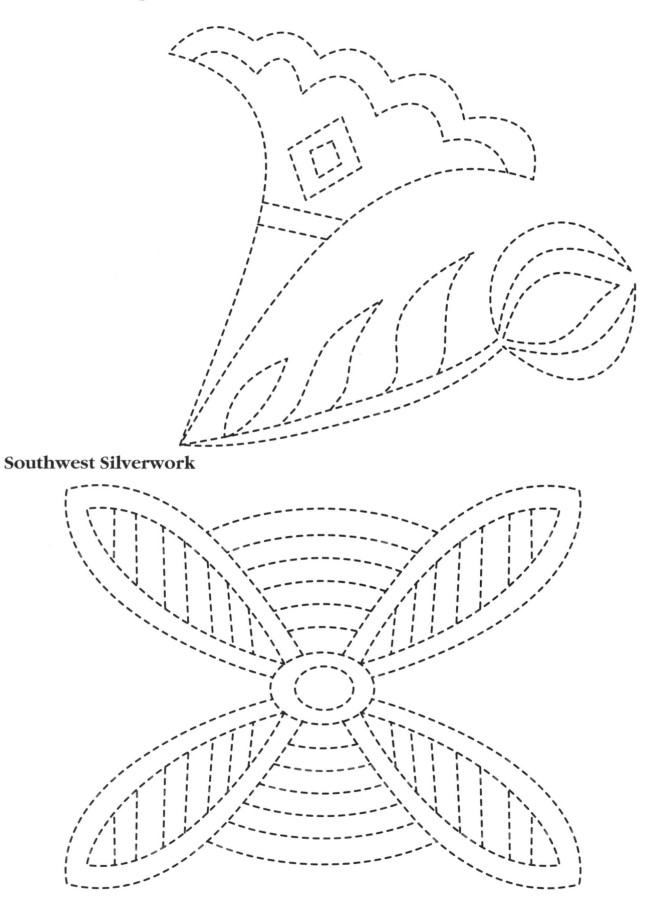

Southwest Silverwork

Southwest Area

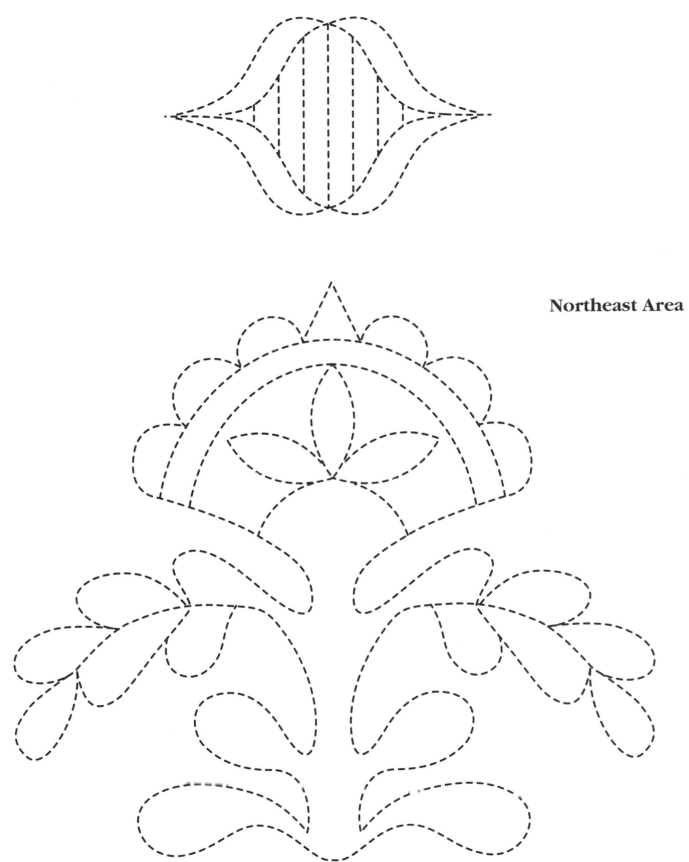

Northeast Area

Montagnais (Northeast Woodland)
Birchbark Basket

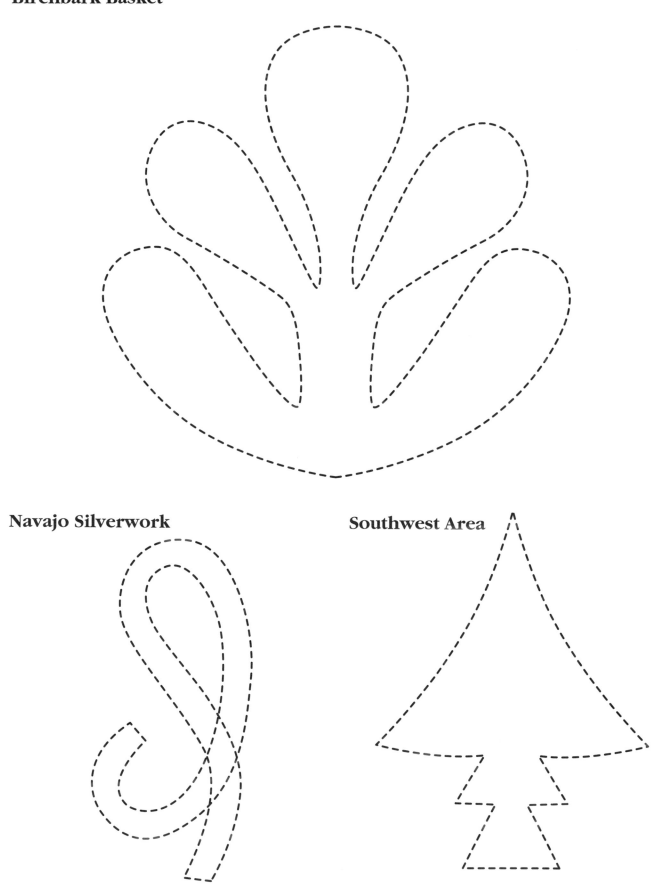

Navajo Silverwork

Southwest Area

Northwest Coast Beadwork

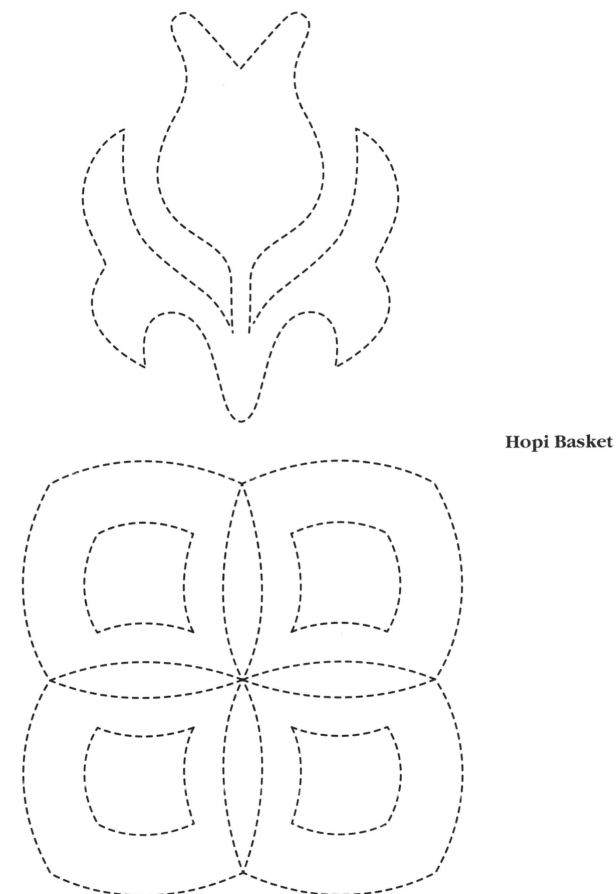

Hopi Basket

Prehistoric Design

Northeast Area

Inuit Harpoon Point

Southeast Beadwork

Southwest Pottery

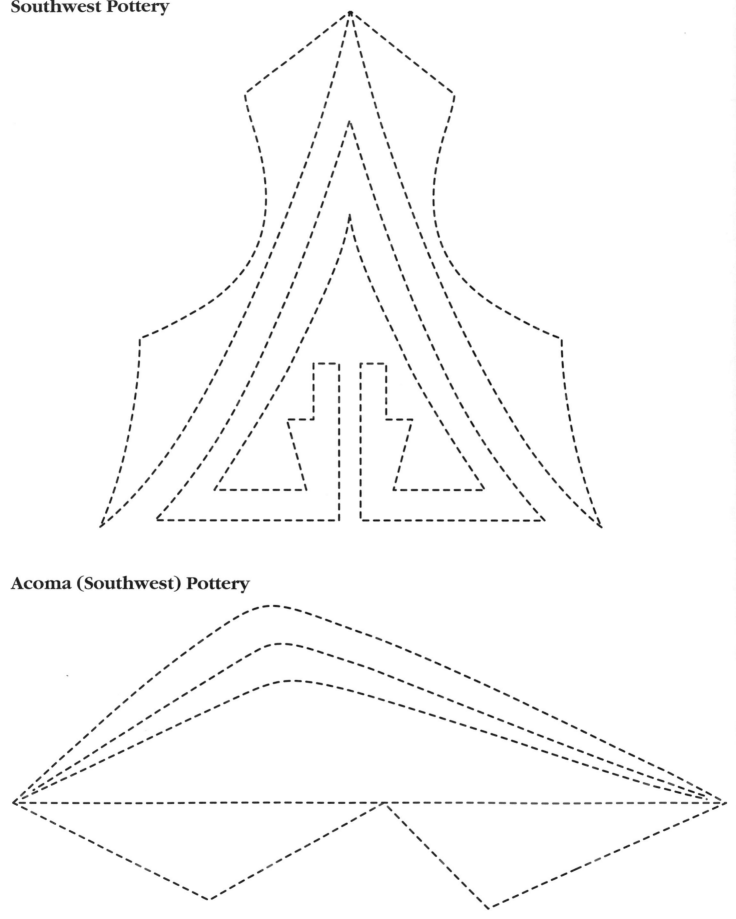

Acoma (Southwest) Pottery

Southwest Area

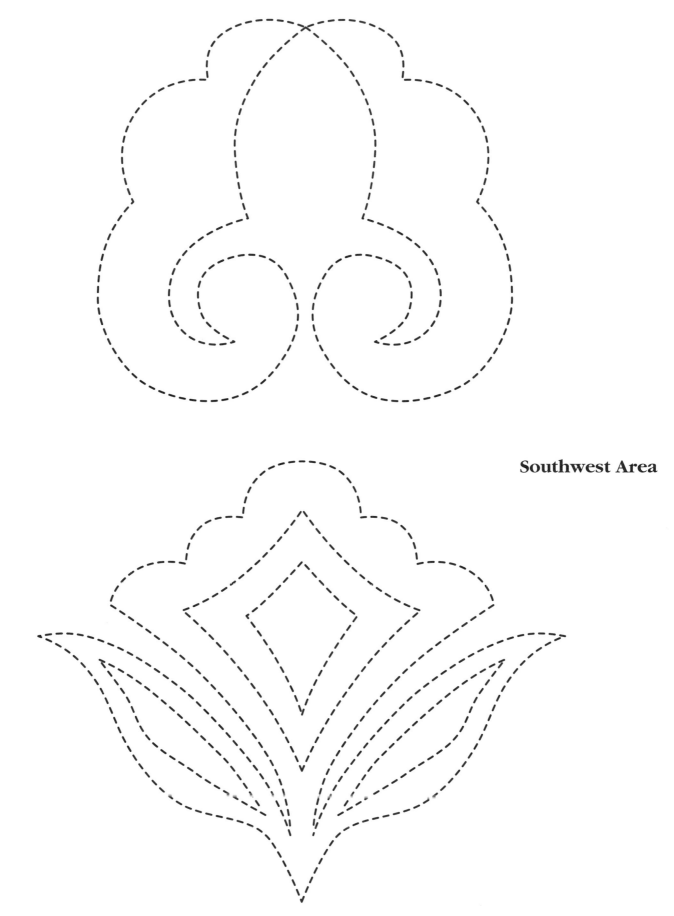

Southwest Area

Southwest Pottery

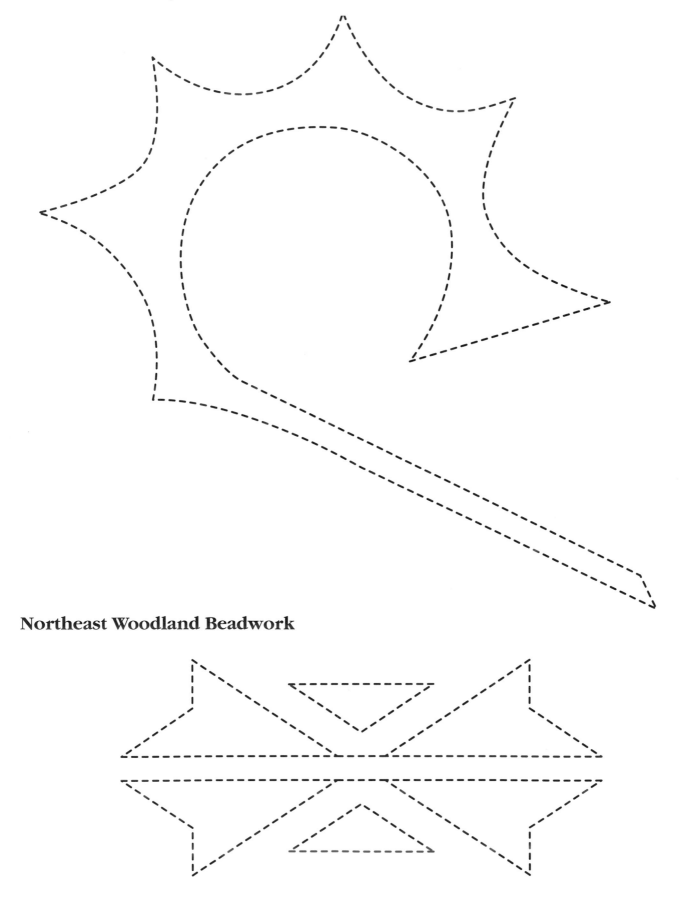

Northeast Woodland Beadwork

Native American Designs 2 – Dr. Joyce Mori

Northwest Coast Beadwork

Zuni Pottery

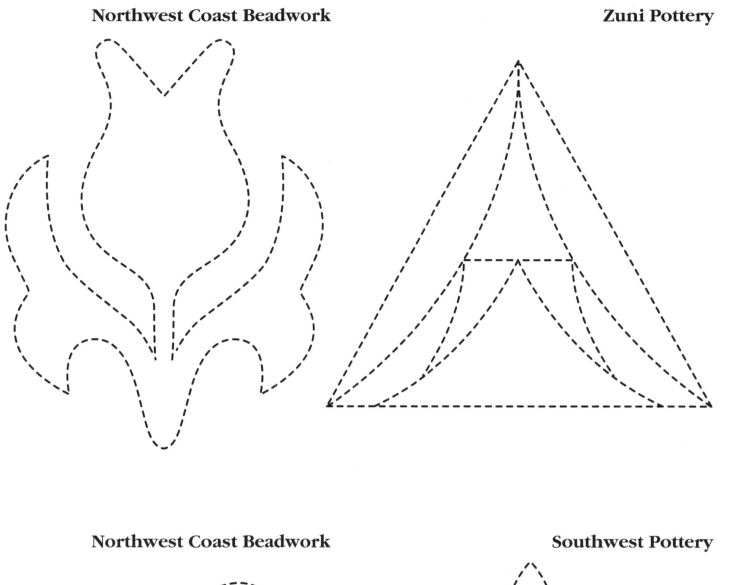

Northwest Coast Beadwork

Southwest Pottery

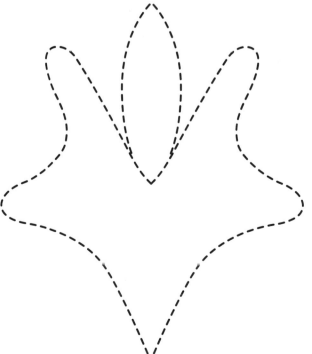

Northeast Woodland Ribbonwork

Northeast Woodland

Southwest Pottery

Northwest Coast

Osage Cradleboard

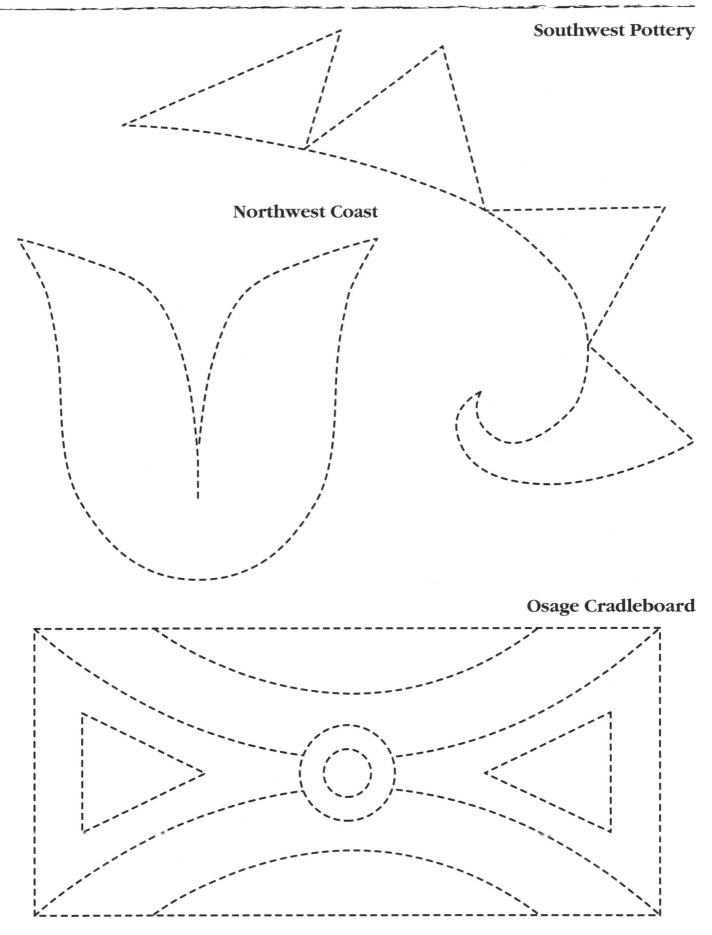

Southwest Design

Full design

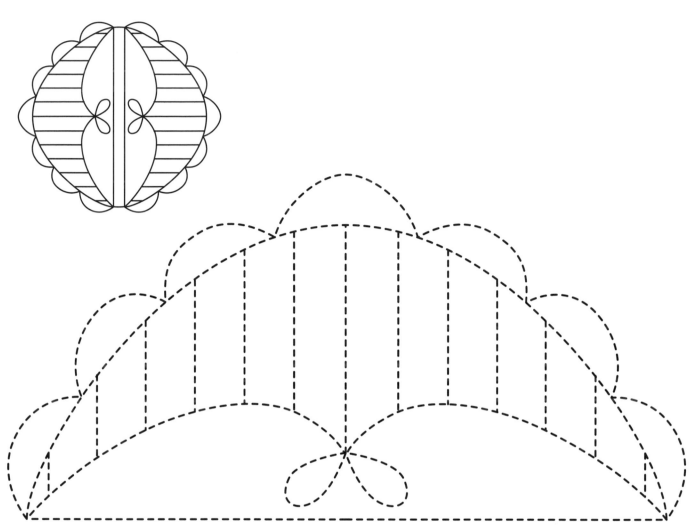

Hopi Pottery

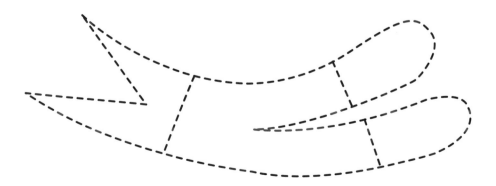

Southwest Pottery

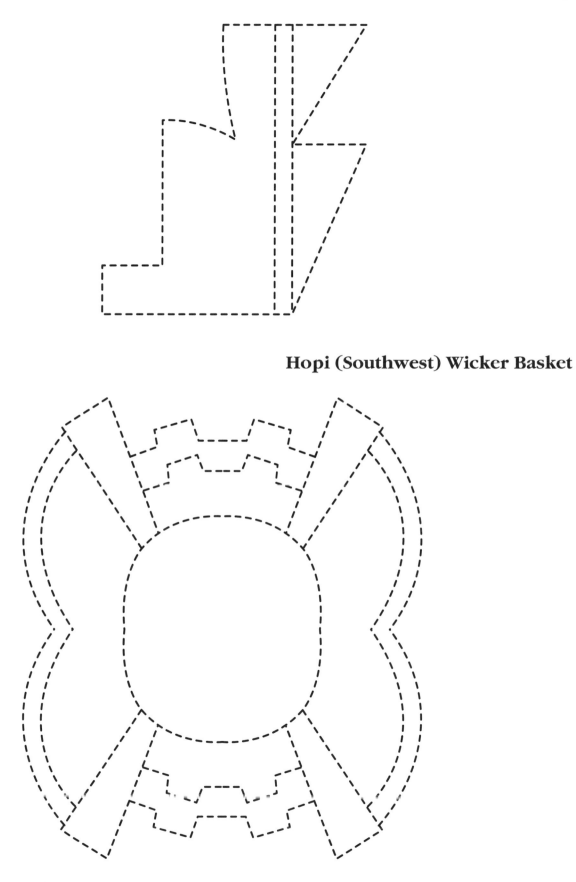

Hopi (Southwest) Wicker Basket

Southwest Corn Maiden

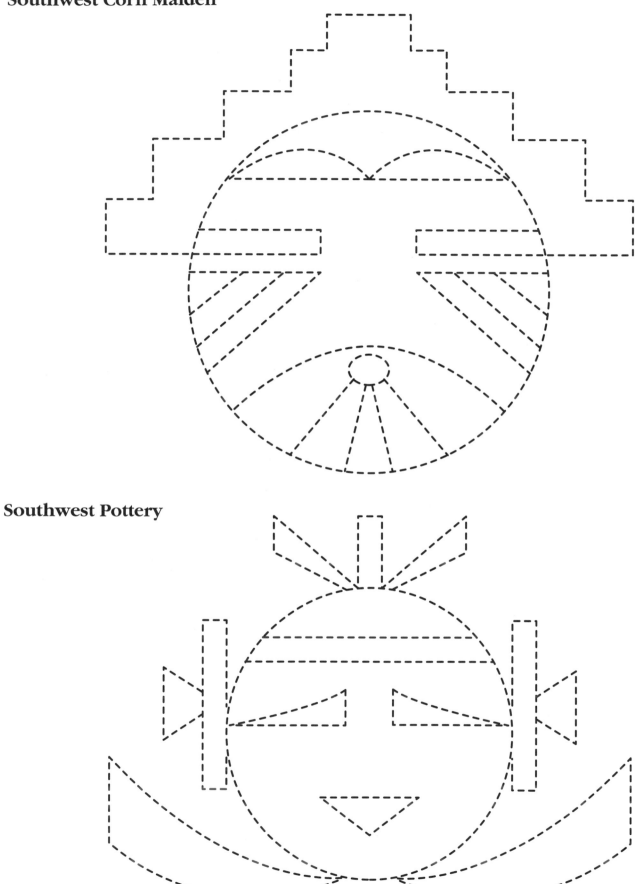

Southwest Pottery

Native American Designs 2 – Dr. Joyce Mori

Northwest Coast Hat

Unknown

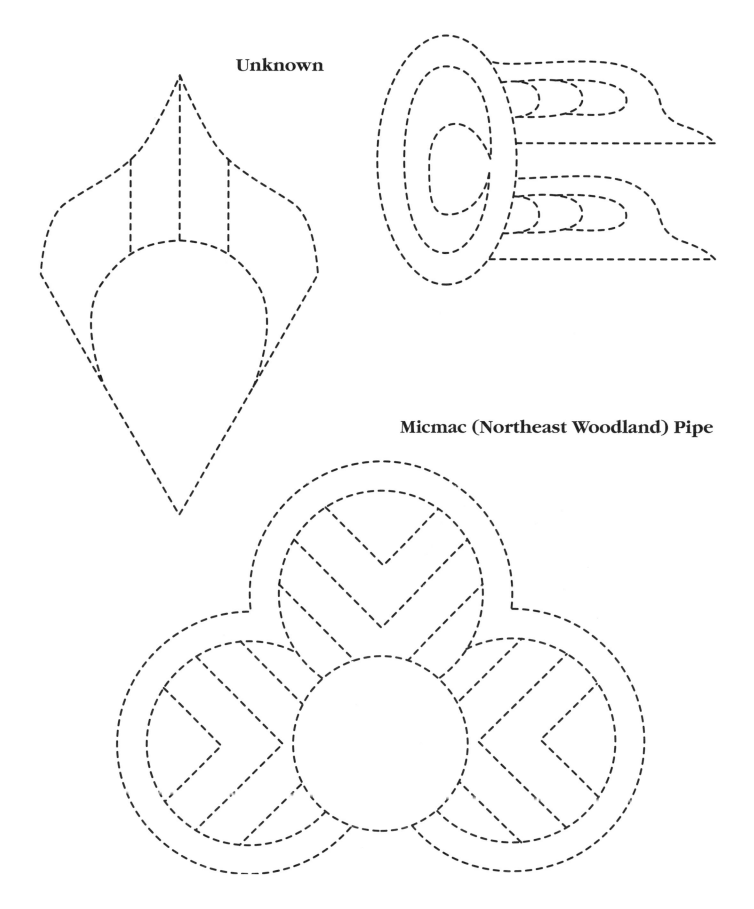

Micmac (Northeast Woodland) Pipe

Pima (Southwest) Basket

Southwest Pottery

Full design

Lakota (Plains) Quillwork

Plateau Quillwork

Prehistoric Southwest Pottery

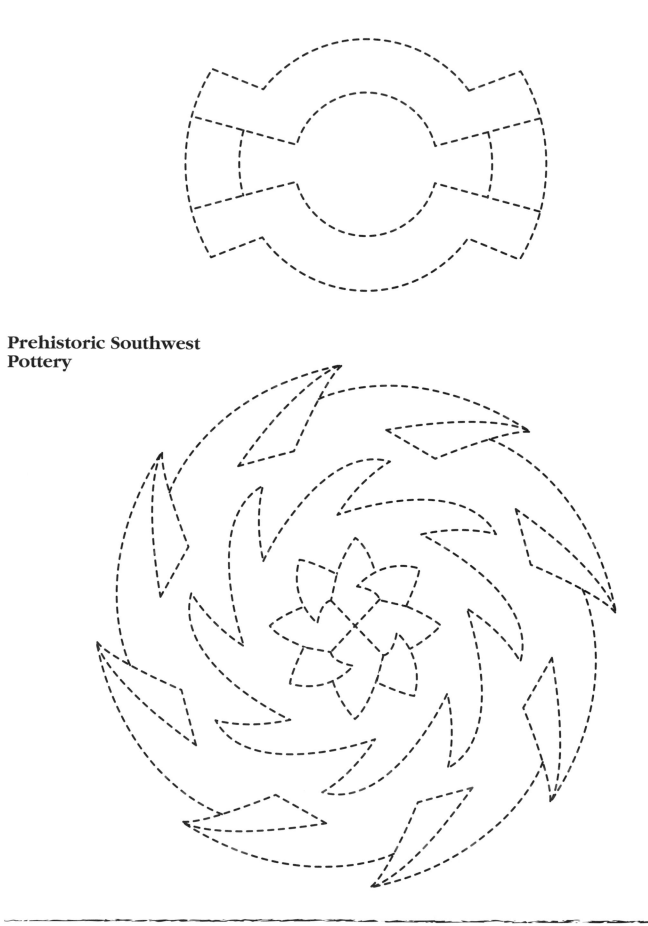

Osage Beadwork   **Southwest Pottery**

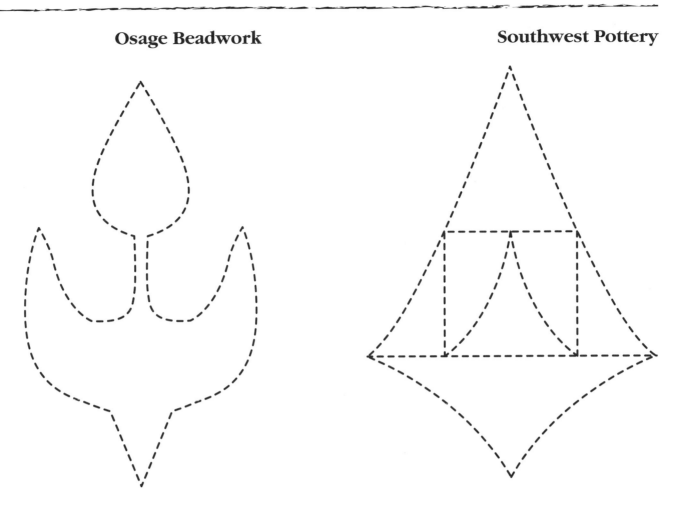

Woodland Beadwork

Hopi (Southwest) Pottery

Southwest Pottery

Hopi (Southwest) Pottery

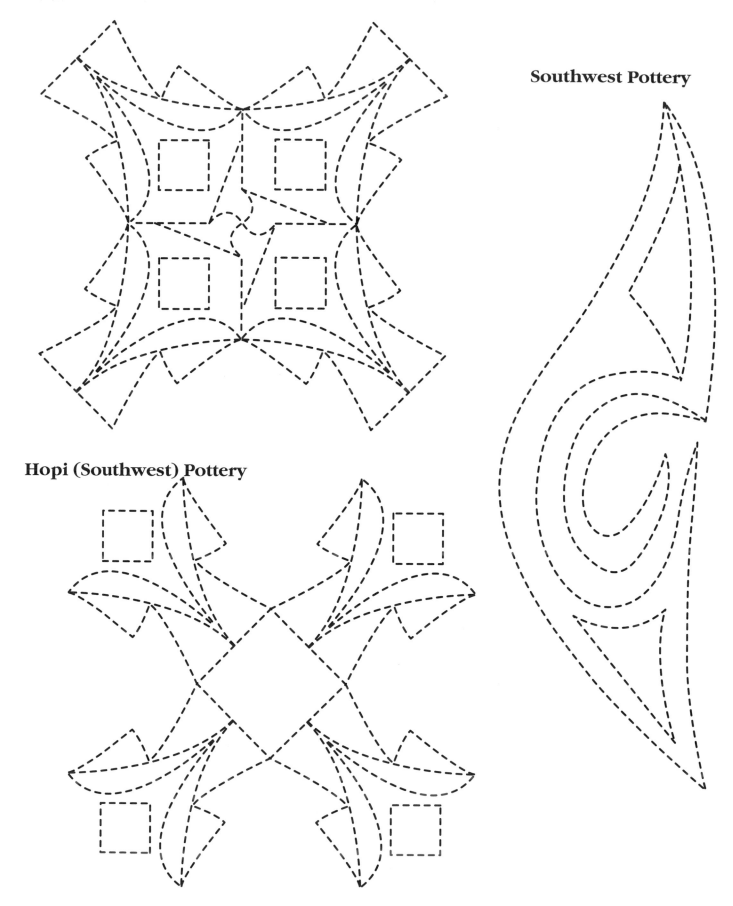

Southwest Silverwork

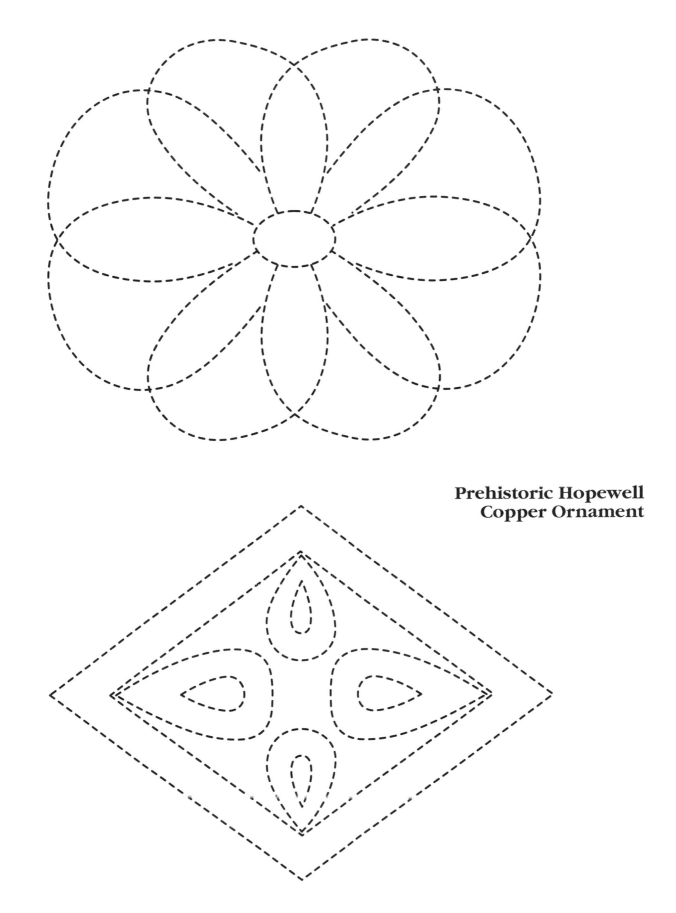

Prehistoric Hopewell
Copper Ornament

Southwest Pottery

Prehistoric Native American Stonework

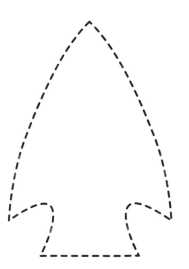

Full design

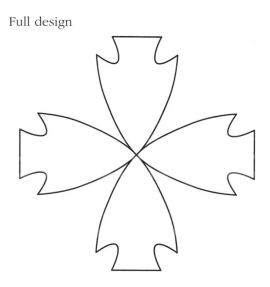

Prehistoric Pottery

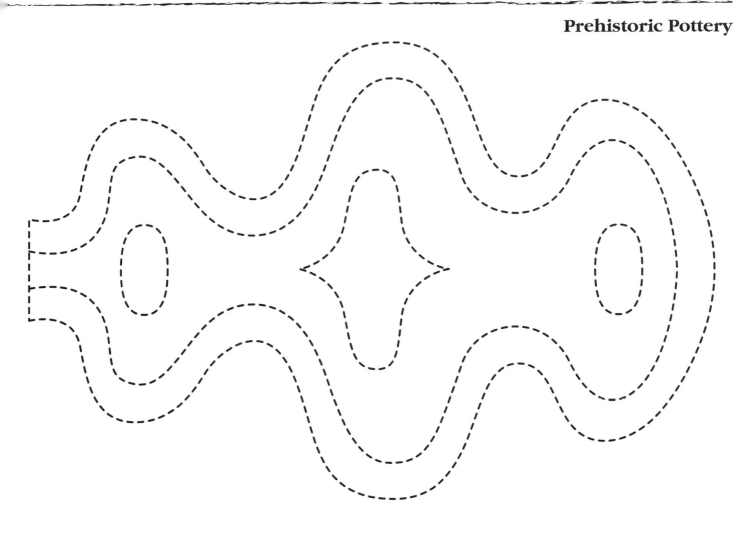

Southwest Pottery

Southwest Pottery

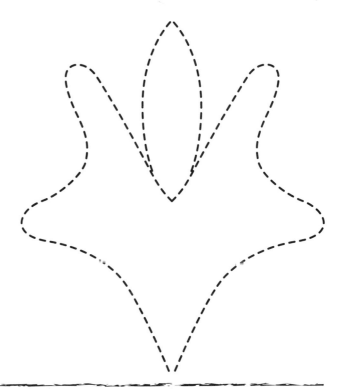

Zia (Southwest) Pottery

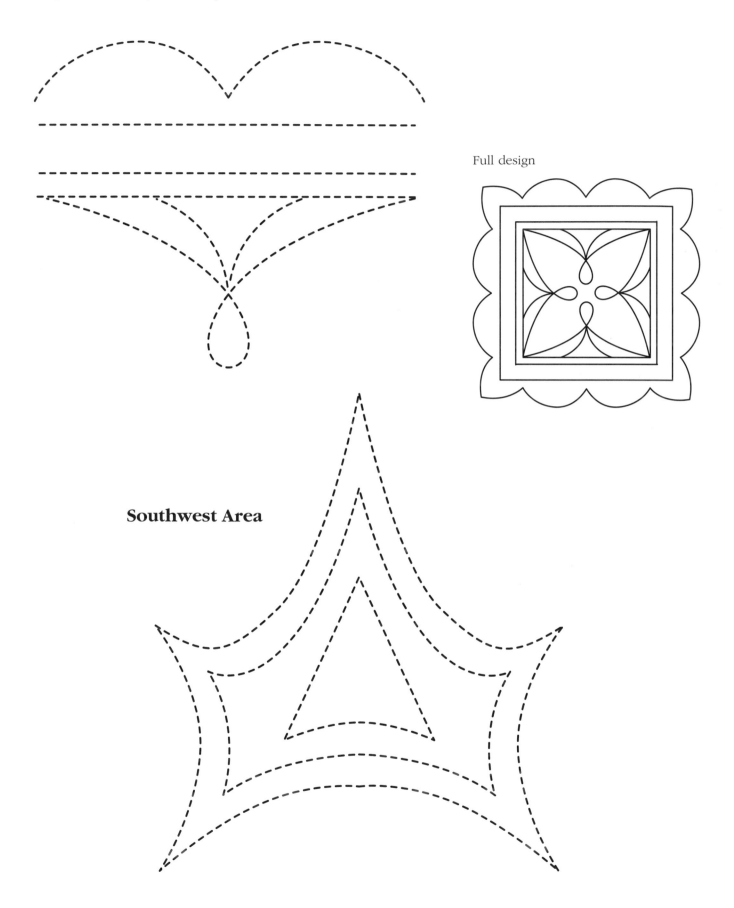

Full design

Southwest Area

Pawnee Design

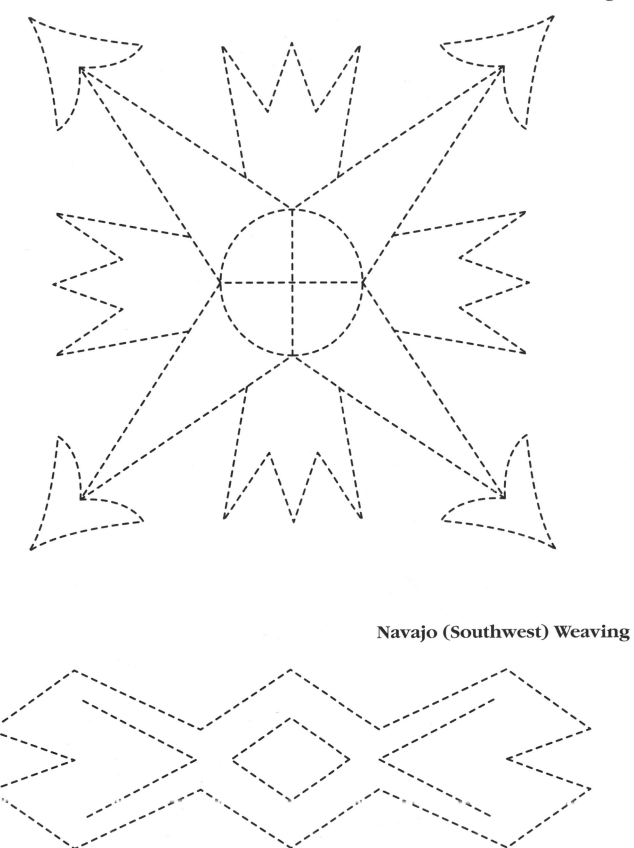

Navajo (Southwest) Weaving

Southwest Design

Northeast Woodland
(Prehistoric)
Shell Gorget

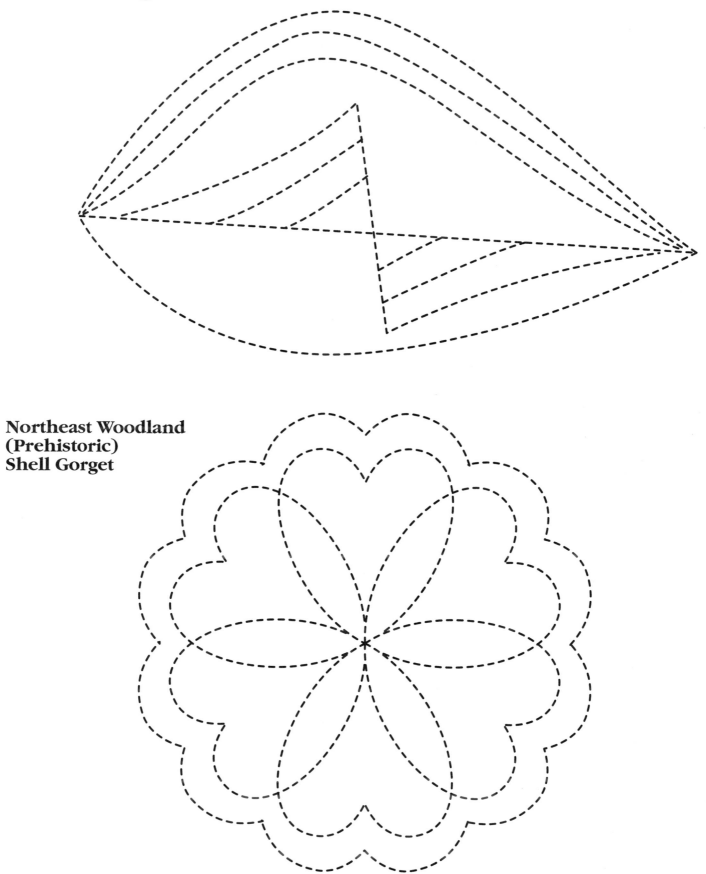

Prehistoric Adena Stonework

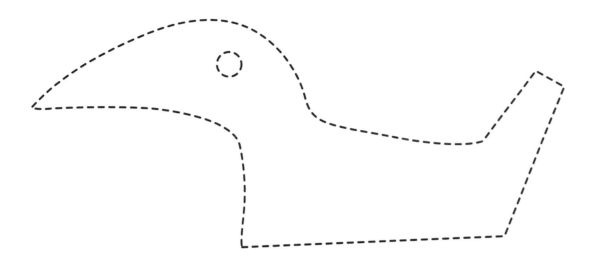

Southwest Pottery

Northwest Coast (Cowichan) Spindle Whorl

Southwest Pottery

Southwest Wooden Tablita

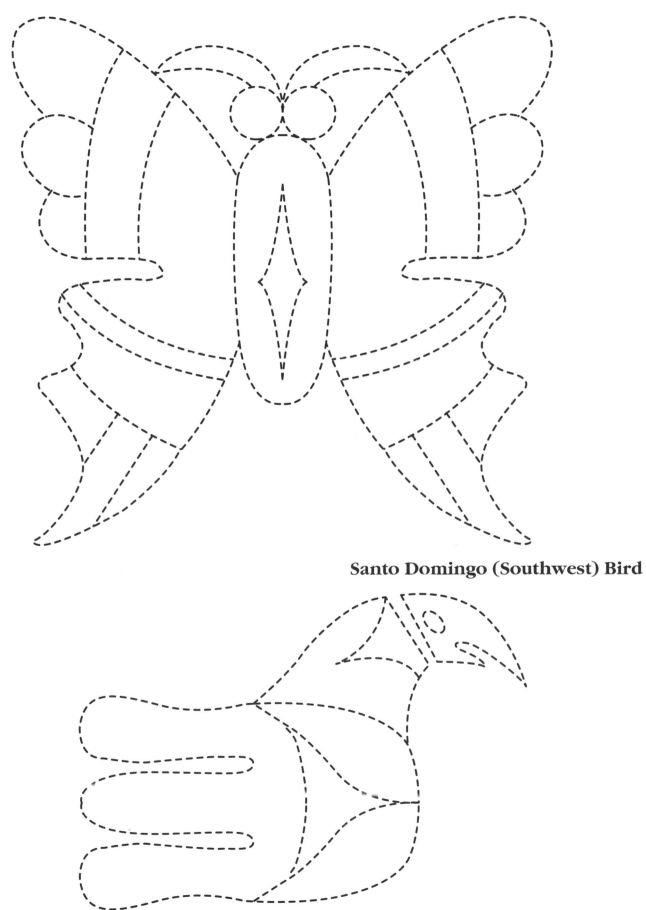

Santo Domingo (Southwest) Bird

Mimbres (Southwest) Pottery

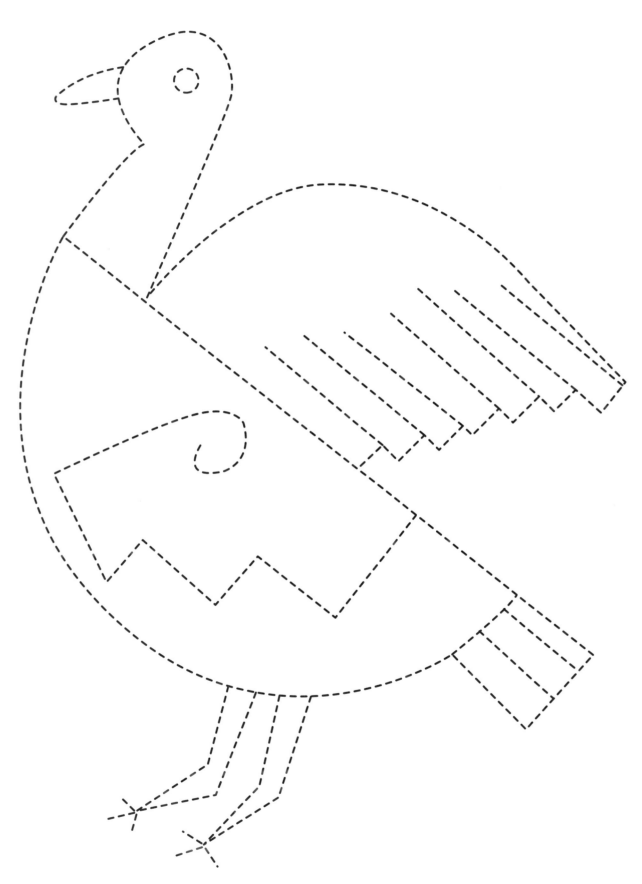

Prehistoric Southwest Pottery

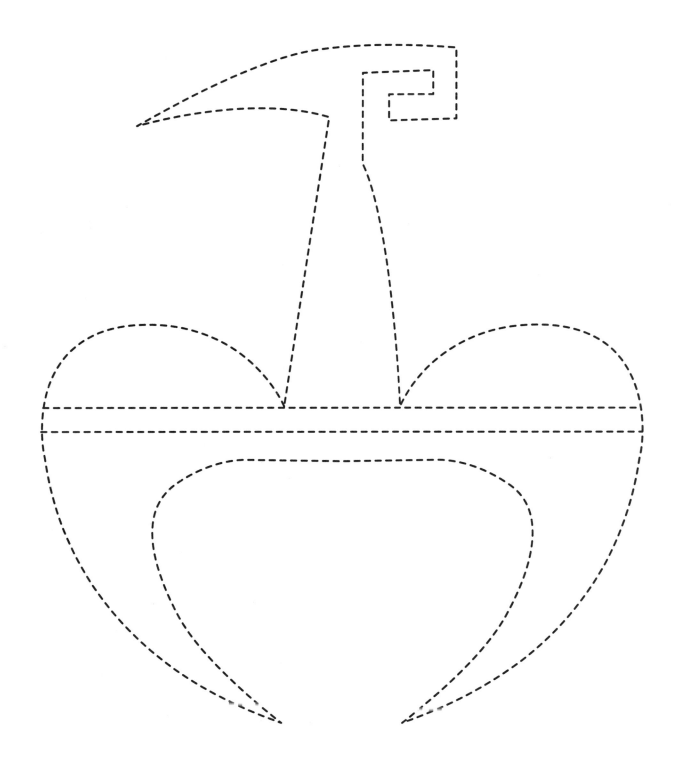

Southwest Area

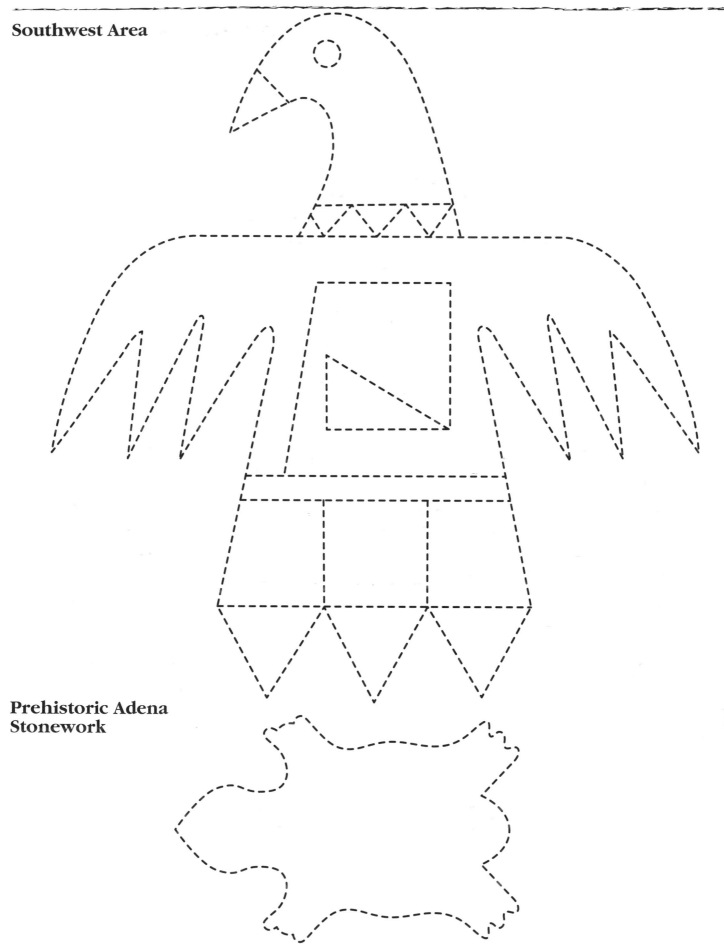

Prehistoric Adena Stonework

Kwakiutl (Northwest Coast) Totem

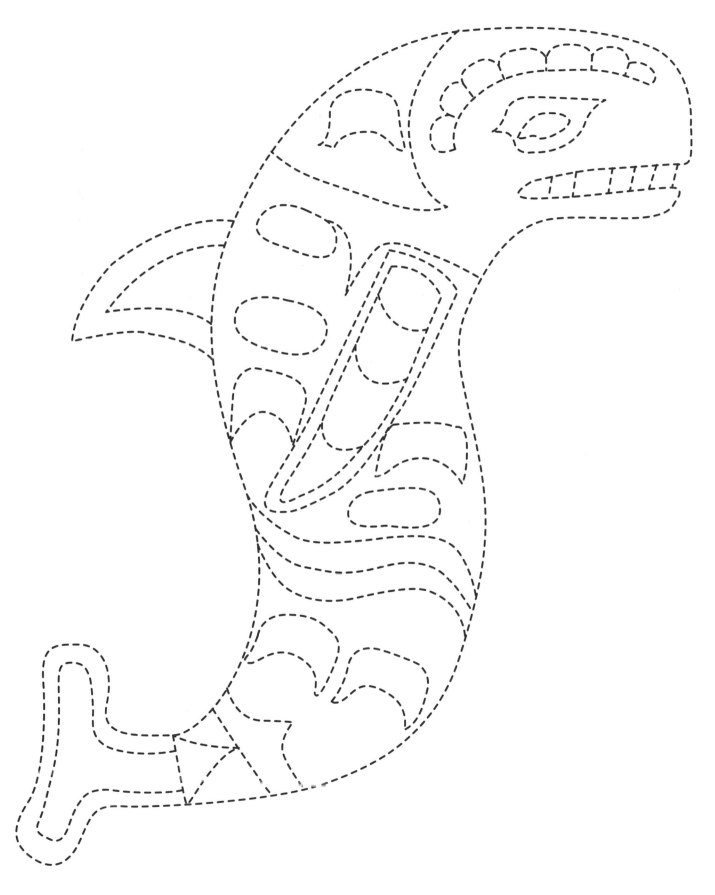

Southwest Design

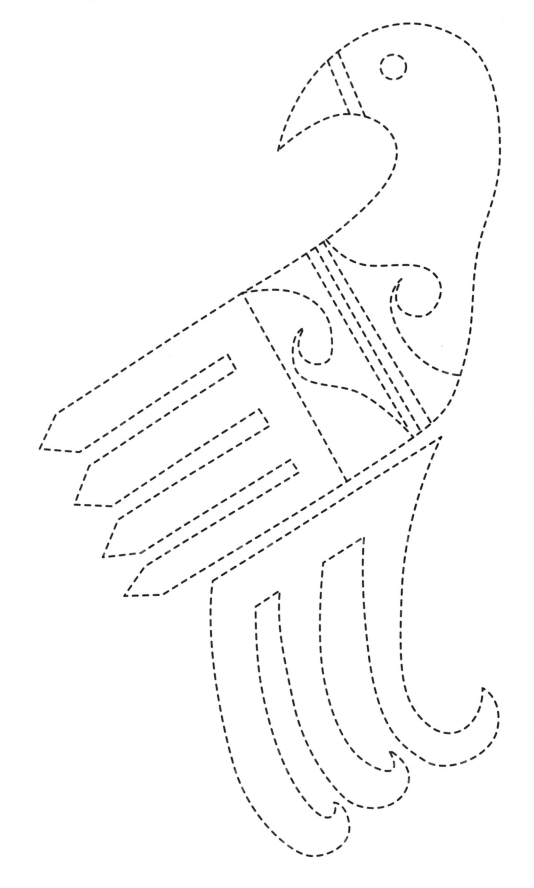

Native American Designs 2 – Dr. Joyce Mori

Prehistoric Mimbres (Southwest) Pottery

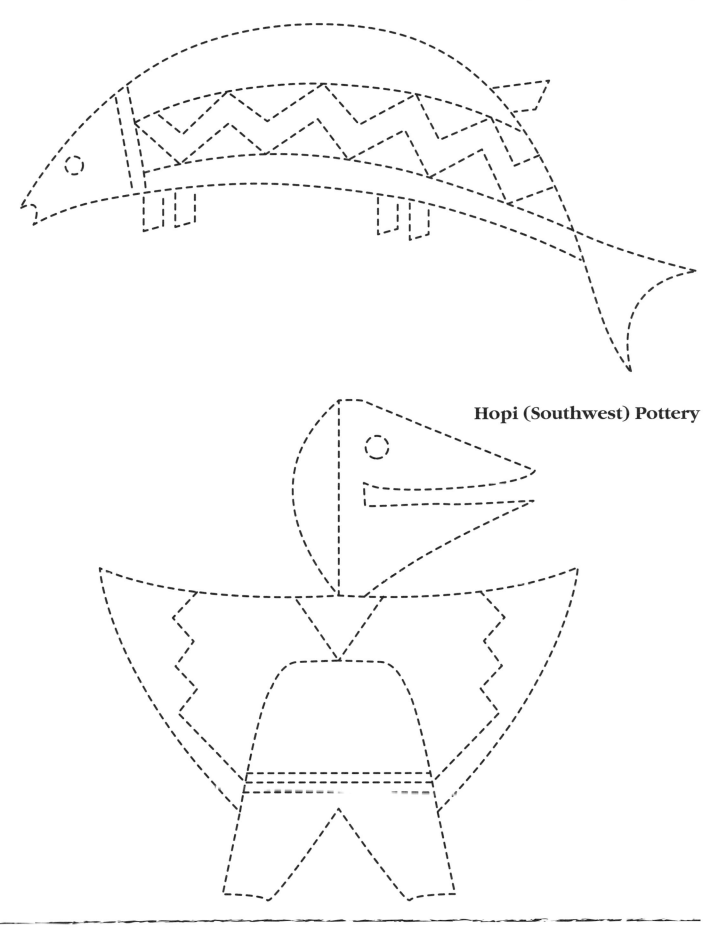

Hopi (Southwest) Pottery

Prehistoric Southeast Design

Zuni (Southwest) Pottery

Northeast Woodland Area

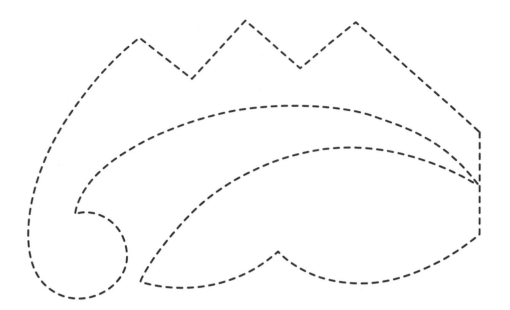

Full design

Southwest Pottery

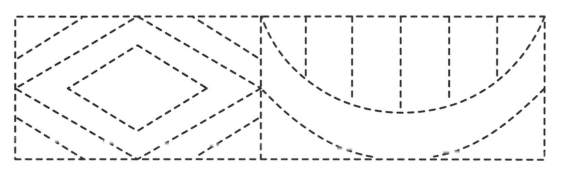

Northwest Coast Beadwork

Corner design

Full design

**Northeast
Woodland**

**Southwest
Pottery**

Midwest Woven Bag

Southwest Weaving

Southwest Pottery

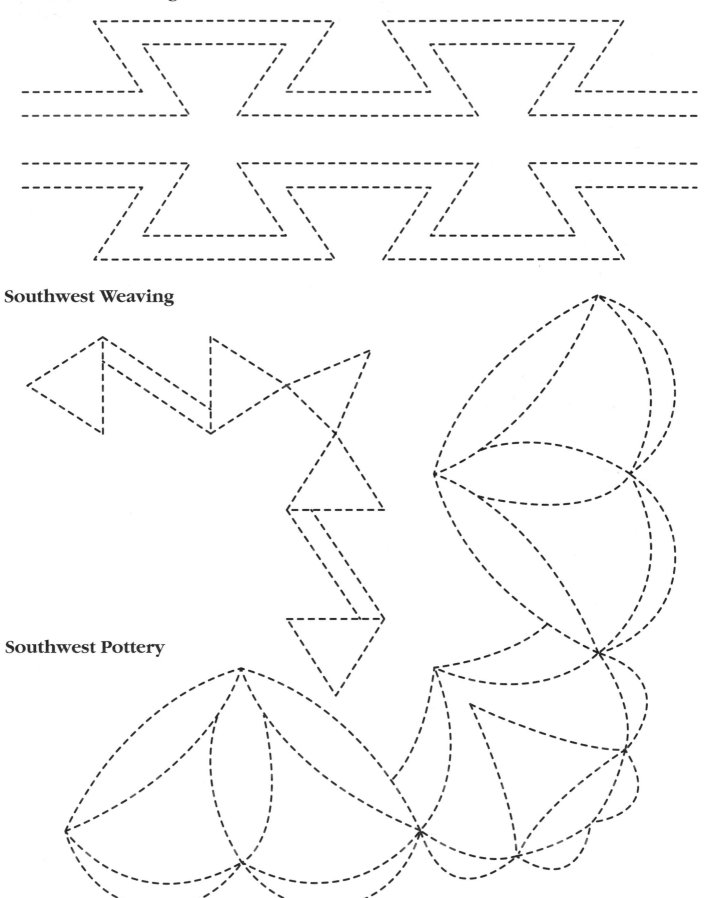

Birchbark Design (Northeast Woodland)

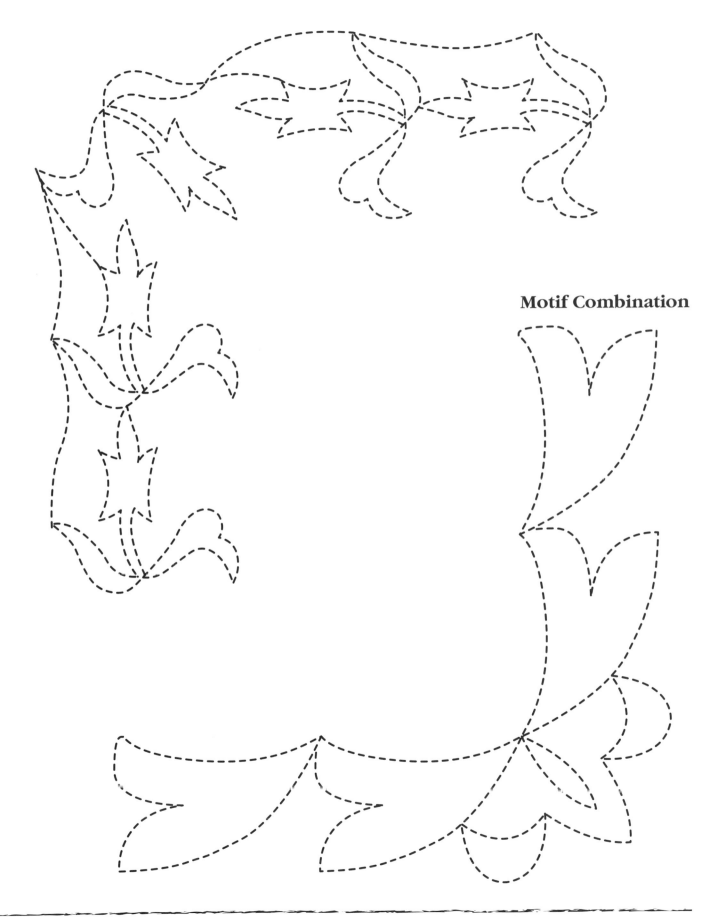

Motif Combination

Sauk (Northeast Woodland) Beadwork

Corner design

Crow (Plains) Beadwork

California/Great Basin Basketry

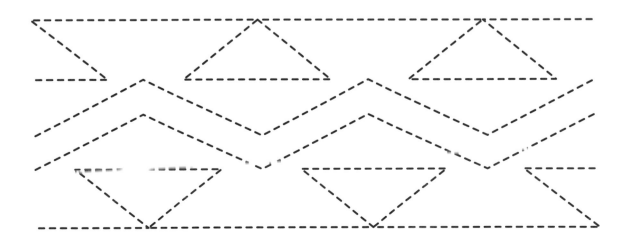

Bonus Patterns

Mandan (Plains) Leggings

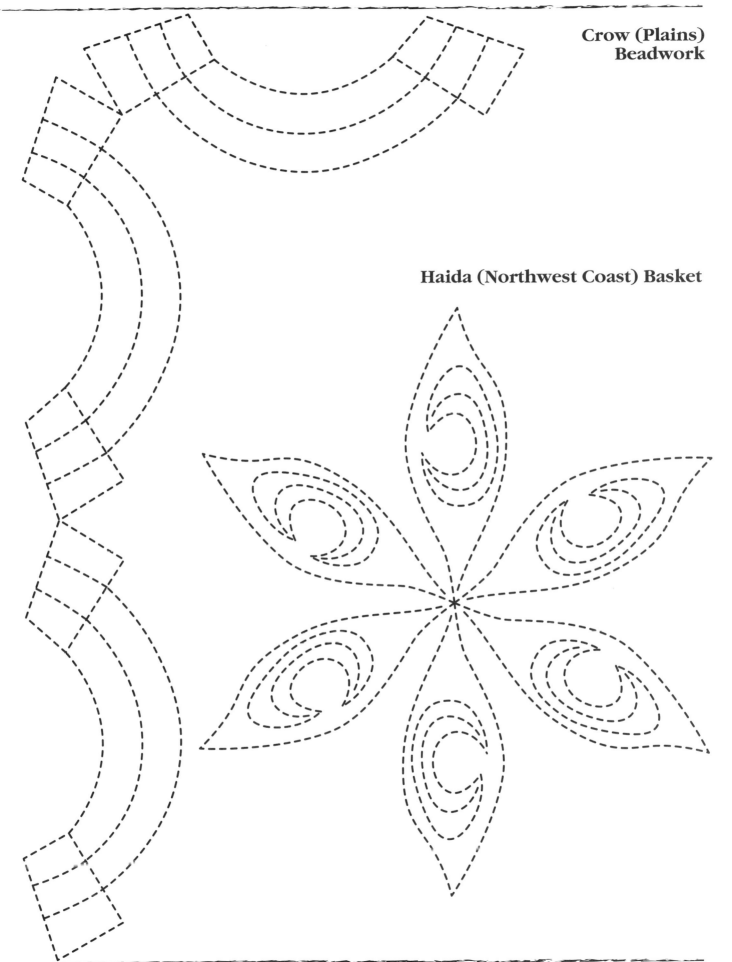

**Crow (Plains)
Beadwork**

Haida (Northwest Coast) Basket

Flathead Beadwork

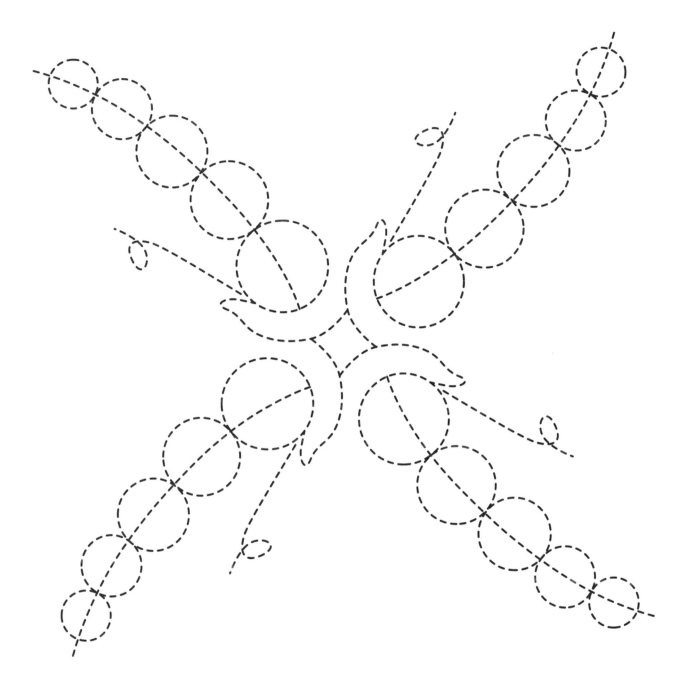

Border design

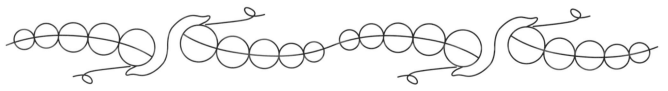

**Tlingit (Northwest Coast)
Beadwork**

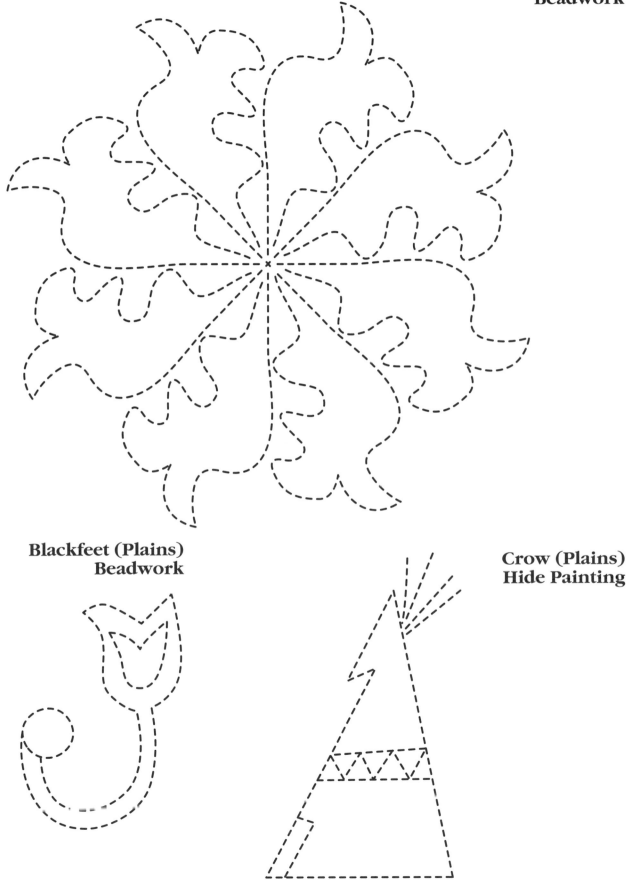

**Blackfeet (Plains)
Beadwork**

**Crow (Plains)
Hide Painting**

Cherokee Beadwork

Aleutian Hat

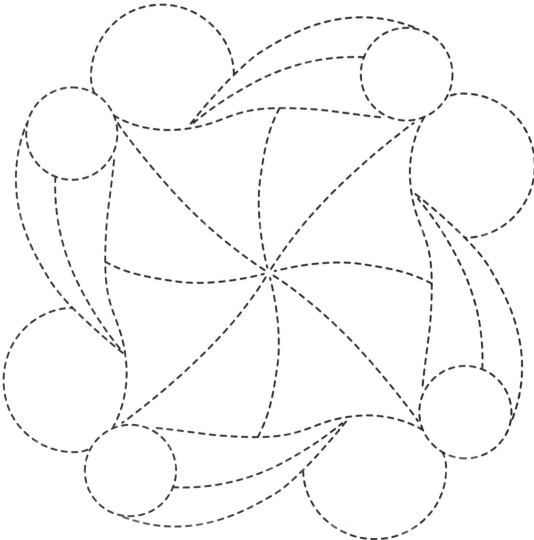

Miwok-Paiute Basket

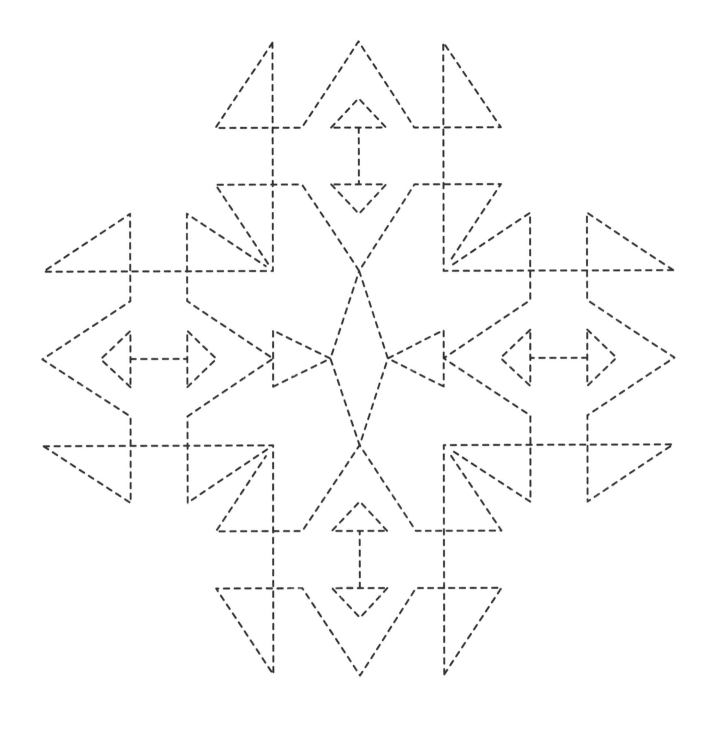

Border design

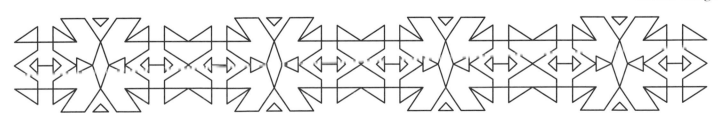

Cheyenne (Plains) Shield

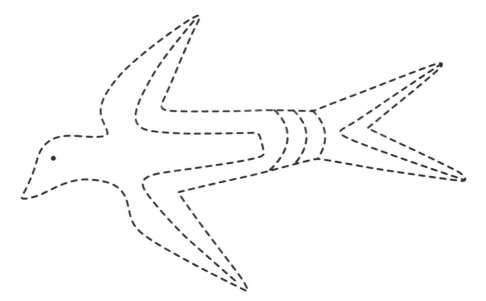

Aleutian Hat

Wasco Twined Bag

Miwok-Paiute Basket

Seminole Patchwork

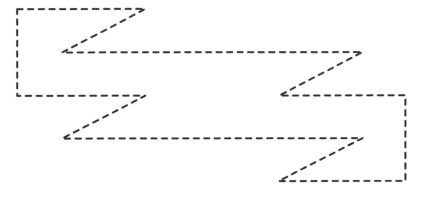

Border design

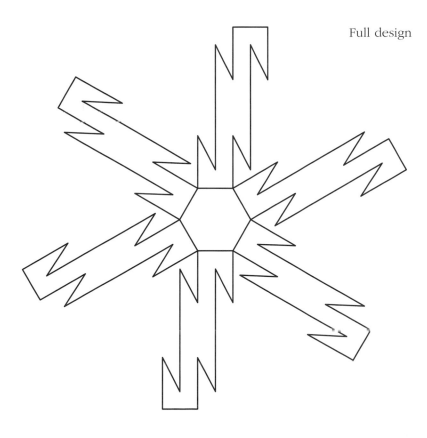

Full design

Lakota (Plains) Beadwork

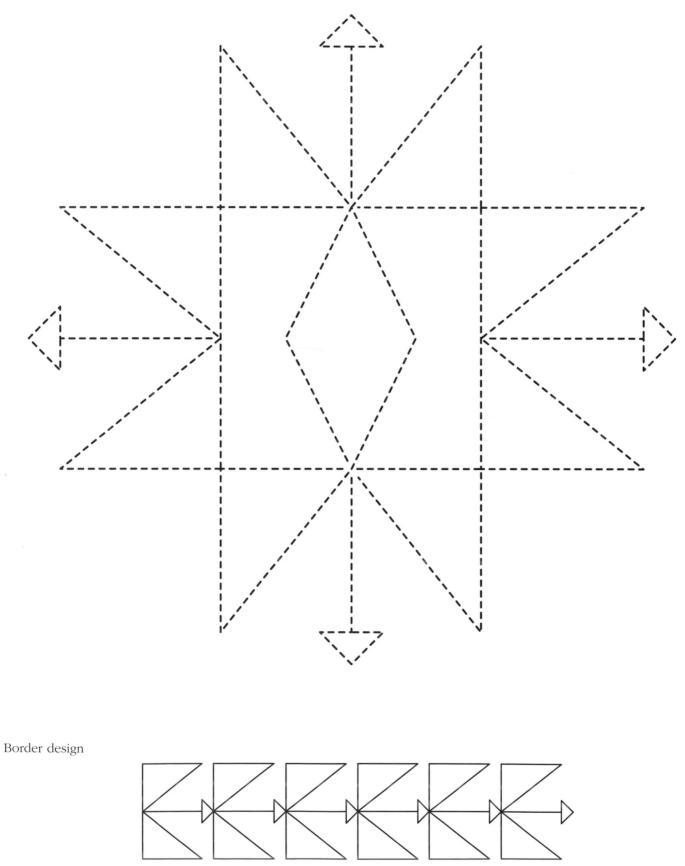

Border design

CONTINUOUS-LINE DESIGNS

Delaware Beadwork

Start

The following patterns were designed for machine quilters, but they can be used by hand quilters as well. Theresa Fleming from Colorado adapted my motifs to continuous-line patterns.

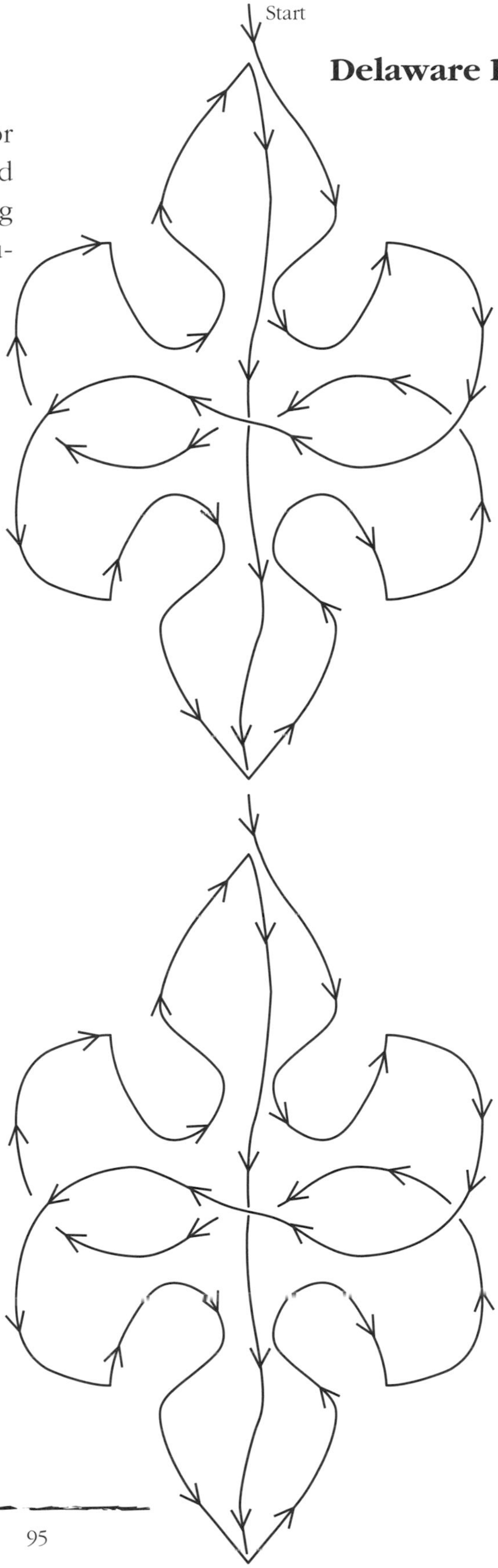

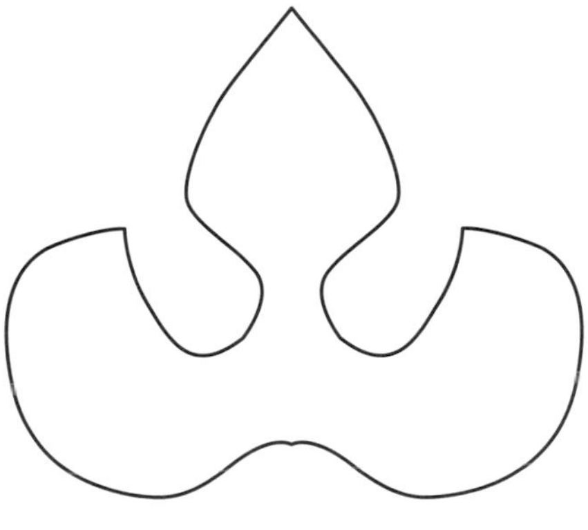

Southwest Silverwork

Start

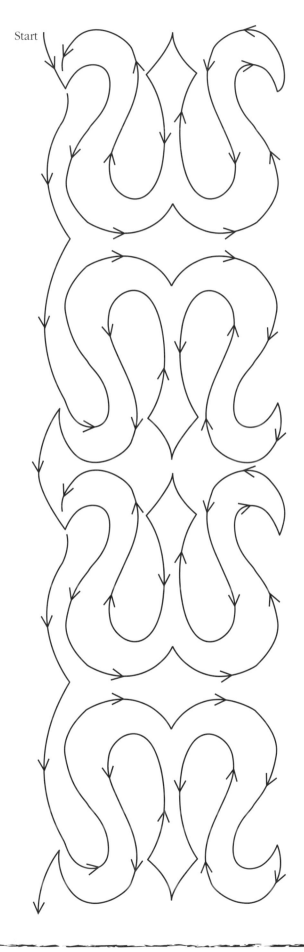

Start

Acoma Pottery

Start

Northeast Woodland Beadwork

Start

Acoma Pottery

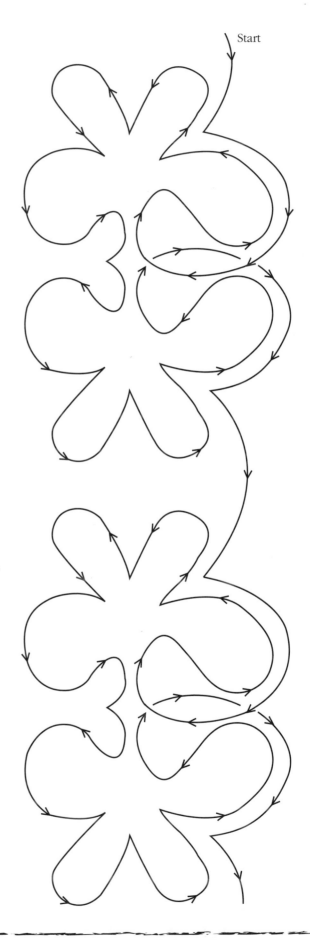

Start

Cree Quillwork

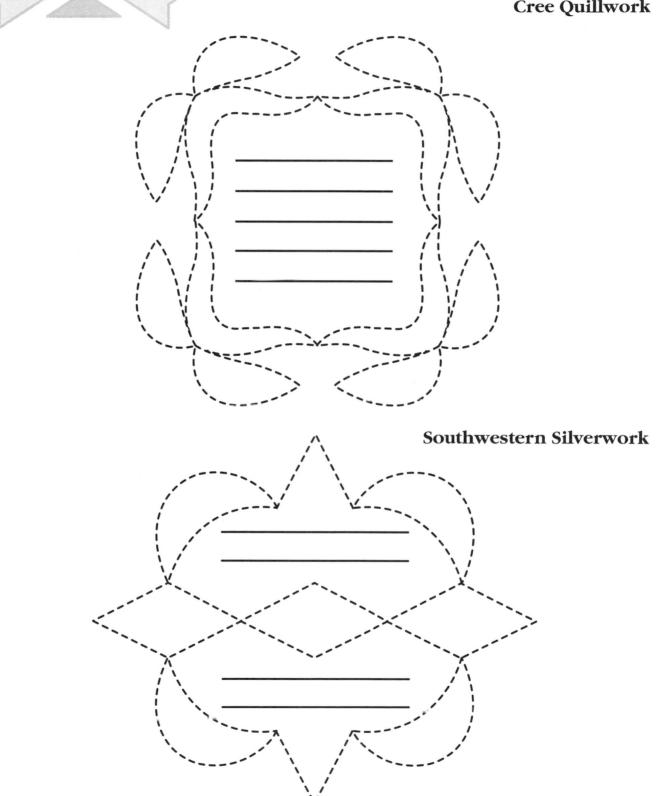

Southwestern Silverwork

Hopi (Southwest)
Wicker Basket Tray

Pima (Southwest) Basket

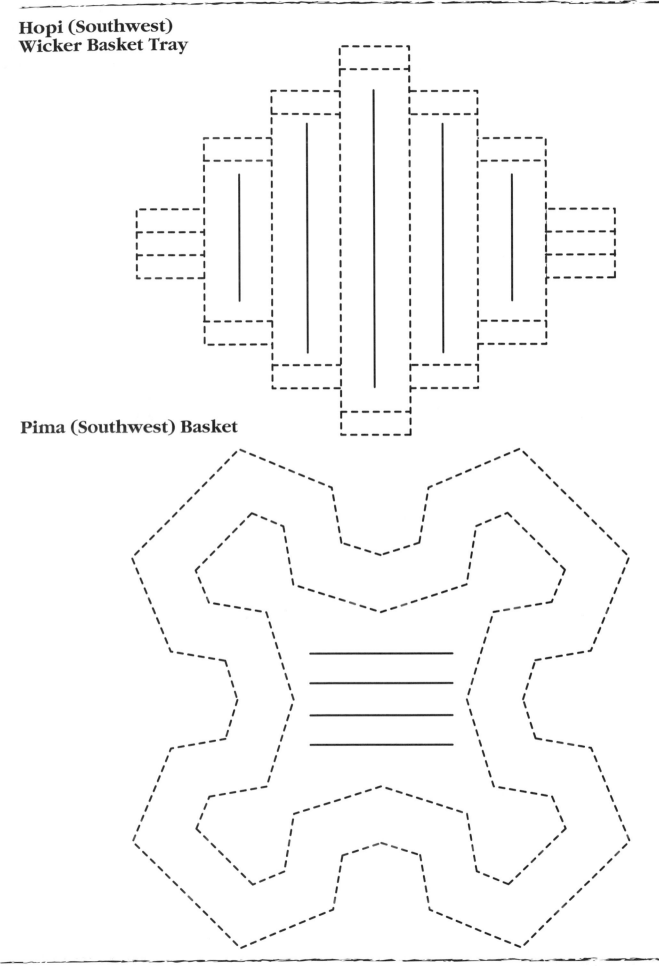

Wallhanging size: 28" x 28"

This wall quilt is the perfect showcase for some of the quilting designs in this book. The center features a quilting design that has been modified for machine appliqué. The quilting designs were completed with two strands of embroidery thread. This was done to make them stand out for photography. The borders of the quilt were adapted from a Navajo rug.

Please refer to the inside cover for a color photograph of the wallhanging.

Fabric Requirements & Cutting

Fabric	Yards	Cuts
☐ Light (beige)	½	64 A rectangles 1½" x 2½"
		4 B squares 1½"
		4 D rectangles 1½" x 4½"
		4 G squares 2½"
☐ Medium (brown print)	½	12 A rectangles 1½" x 2½"
		36 B squares 1½"
		20 C rectangles 1½" x 3½"
		4 E rectangles 1½" x 6½"
		4 F rectangles 2½" x 3½"
☐ Dark (brown)	¼	16 A rectangles 1½" x 2½"
		16 D rectangles 1½" x 4½"
☐ Sherbet	⅓	4 D rectangles 1½" x 4½"
		4 H rectangles 2½" x 6½"
		1 J square 6½"
Light orange	fat quarter*	2 I squares 8½"
Sage green	fat quarter*	2 I squares 8½"
Rust	10" square	Iroquois Silverwork pattern, Section A, pg. 111
Dark rust	7" square	Iroquois Silverwork pattern, Section B
Black binding	¼	3 strips 1⅛" x 42"
Backing	1	
Batting	32" square	

*If you are embroidering the blocks, ½ yard of fabric is required. The squares should be cut to 12" and the designs embroidered prior to piecing the quilt.

Quilt Assembly

1. Refer to the unit diagrams, page 105, to make the following units: four of unit 1, eight of unit 2, four of unit 3, and four of unit 4.

2. Refer to the quilt assembly diagram, page 106, to sew the units and squares together in five horizontal rows.

3. Using your favorite appliqué method, attach Section A of the Iroquois Silverwork pattern to the center of the quilt top. Then appliqué Section B over Section A.

4. Baste the quilt top, batting, and backing. Quilt (the designs in this quilt are on the following pages). Bind and label your quilt.

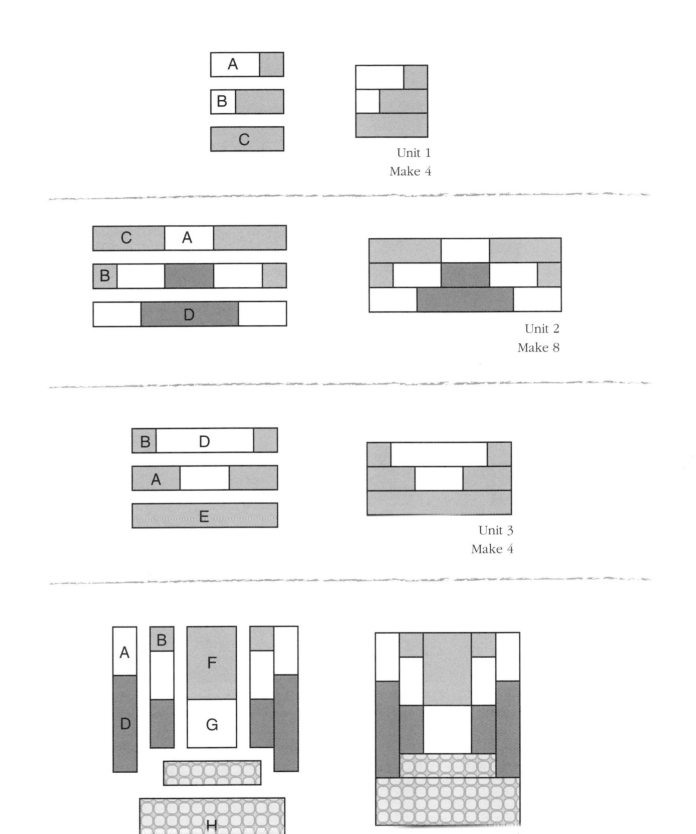

Unit 1
Make 4

Unit 2
Make 8

Unit 3
Make 4

Unit 4
Make 4

Unit 1   Unit 2   Unit 3

Unit 4

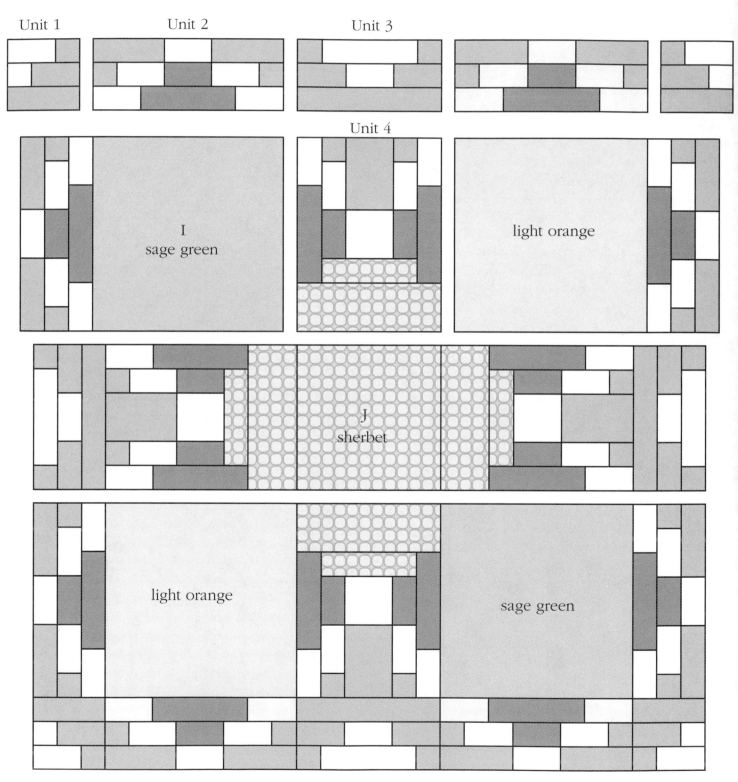

I
sage green

light orange

J
sherbet

light orange

sage green

Quilt assembly

Pawnee Design

Plains Cree Beadwork

Iroquois (Northeast Woodland) Silverwork

Full design

Reverse at center

B

A

For turned-edge appliqué, add a 3/16" allowance.

ABOUT
THE AUTHOR

Specializing in diverse designs and cultures, Dr. Joyce Mori has been quilting for over 15 years. This is her sixth book for the American Quilter's Society. She has written over 75 articles and 13 books on quilting subjects. Her work has been exhibited in galleries and quilt shows, as well as public buildings and private collections.

Adapting motifs from different cultural items, Joyce creates quilting designs and generates ideas for quilt projects. Joyce's interest in other cultures comes from her educational training and her Ph.D. in anthropology.

She finds that quilting is a wonderful outlet for creative expression and has collaborated on some quilted pieces with her adult daughter, Susan. Joyce lives in Illinois with her husband, John.